ACCLAIM FOR "MY SC

MW01235095

"This book shows the human dimension of today's military. It is a real testimony to reality and what sacrifice is all about. All who appreciate their freedom should read it."

LTG James D. Thurman – Brian's
Commanding General in Iraq

"What a gutsy lady, holding it all together when Brian needed her most, and what a blessing Mary is. This story really is a huge eye-opener, even to somebody like me who thought she knew it all but didn't know the half of it…"

Sal March – A British Supporter of our Military

"I think Roberta does a wonderful job of very honestly capturing her emotions, feelings and such as she walks the walk of a Mother whose son's life has been changed forever due to a tragedy of war."

Amy Moore – An Army Wife and Mother

"I really enjoyed the book. Anyone who has had, or has, or may have a loved one in Iraq or Afghanistan would want to read the story."

Bob Collins – Retired Coach and
Cold War Marine

"Roberta writes with compassion and love and conveys these feelings to the reader. It has a journal quality about it but she has documented it well for continuity. I came to admire her and to feel compassion and sorrow for her son's terrible injuries. I couldn't put it down."

Lynn Kruger – A Patriotic Mother

"MY SON IS ALIVE..."

OTHER BOOKS BY DEEDS PUBLISHING

War Stories – Utah Beach to Pleiku

Operation Iraqi Freedom I: A Year in the Sunni Triangle

What Now, Lieutenant?

The Sooner the Better

You Don't Know Jack... or Jerry

www.deedspublishing.com

"MY SON IS ALIVE..."

*A Mother's Loving Support
of her Son Wounded in Iraq*

Roberta Quimby

Deeds Publishing
Marietta, GA

All pictures, unless otherwise noted, are from the personal collection of the author.

Pictures on pages 139 and 140 are copyright of The Patriot Ledger (MA). Photos by Greg Derr. Used with permission.

Pictures on page 153 used with permission of Homes For Our Troops.

Cover design and layout by Ali Grasty and Jeff McKay

Printed in the United States of America
Published by Deeds Publishing, Marietta, GA

First Edition, 2007

Books are available in quantity for promotional or premium use. For information write Deeds Publishing, PO Box 682212, Marietta, GA 30068 or www.deedspublishing.com

ISBN 0-9776018-4-6

TABLE OF CONTENTS

DEDICATION

To Brian and all the wounded warriors, their families,
and the staff who love and care for them.

---

*To help support our wounded warriors, ten percent of the profits from
the sale of this book will be donated to organizations supporting
wounded warriors.*

ACKNOWLEDGMENTS

I first thank Brian for allowing me to write and publish this book. He has and continues to inspire me with his strength, courage, and determination.

My husband, Chet, has been extremely supportive throughout this ordeal. He kept the house running and the Jacuzzi in tip top shape while I was gone.

Cassie and Haley, my daughter and granddaughter, I am not sure I would have made it without the two of you. You both gave me strength, joy, and laughter when I needed it the most.

Faye and Sandy, my buddies at Walter Reed, gave me advice and plenty of hugs when they were needed the most.

Mary Long gave up her home and family to move to Washington to become Brian's non-medical attendant. But she was much more than that. She became his love, his Mary. She has been strong and protective of Brian. I felt at peace leaving him with her. Thank you, Mary, for giving me that peace.

Brian's Dad, Paul, is a Boston Firefighter – they always take care of their own. The fundraiser they put together for Brian was amazing. The money they raised will surely give him security for many years. No one knows what the future holds for Brian, but having that financial cushion will certainly make his life easier. Thank you all for doing that. He may not become a Boston Firefighter, but you all know that he is one of you in spirit.

The Whitman American Legion Post 22, the Whitman VFW, and the Hanson American Legion Post 226 all came together and raised a tremendous amount of money for Brian. All invited him to become a member of their organizations. He is looking forward to getting to know all of these wonderful people when he comes home. Thank you for "watching his back". He knows when all is said and done, you will still be there for him.

The Hanson Veteran's Agent, Bob Arsenault, has been a great source of help and advice. He was instrumental in getting the handicapped ramp built for Brian. The local carpenters union really came through and did a great job. "Homes for Our Troops" is building a home for Brian, with construction to begin soon. An offshoot of Homes for Our Troops is building a handicapped bathroom downstairs for Brian to use when he is here with us. Thanks for helping to make Brian's life easier.

To all the people of the Hanson Whitman Military Support Group, a huge thank you. Thank you for supporting me and thank you for supporting all the troops who are in Iraq. Brian told me how grateful he was to receive the care packages that you sent him. Keep up your good work – it is truly appreciated.

Thanks to all the people I work with at Mark-It Market, for the support and encouragement you have given me. You are the best group of people I have ever worked with. Your care and concern mean the world to me. You have rejoiced with me in Brian's accomplishments and felt sorrow with his setbacks. Your patience with the never ending pictures of Haley and Brian has been amazing.

To my family and my friends, I thank you for your loving support – with a special thank you to Ellen and Robin. When I needed someone to talk to while at Walter Reed, you were both there for me. Ellen, you always made me smile and laugh and for that, I will be forever grateful. Robin, I don't know if you realize how much your letters and packages meant to Brian when he was in Iraq. He talks about your support of him often. Thank you.

Bob Babcock, thank you for everything. You were a lifeline when Brian was deployed the first time and you were there the second time. When he was injured, you were a source of comfort and wisdom. Your emails gave me hope. Thank you for being my editor and my publisher. I respect and appreciate all that you have done for me. Thanks also to the early readers you selected who gave us feedback to help make this book as good as we can make it.

And all my email recipients – you all know who you are. You will never know how much sending all of those emails to you meant to me. They made me feel like I was in contact with you – my family and my friends. I did not feel so alone when I was writing the emails to all of you. Thank you all for the thoughts and the prayers that you sent Brian and me. I truly believe we are where we are because of them.

And finally, to the memory of my parents and Brian and Cassie's grandparents, Russell and Nancy Frye. You are missed more than words could ever express.

MY SON IS ALIVE...

INTRODUCTION

"On June 8, 2006, while serving my country on a second tour of duty in Iraq, I met my fate in the form of a deadly explosion. My name is Sergeant Brian Fountaine - I am an American Soldier.

"On that fateful day, an Improvised Explosive Device (IED) detonated under the Humvee I was commanding, seriously injuring myself, as well as my driver. Little did I know but that one horrific day wouldn't compare to the next year of blood, sweat, and tears. I truly believe that I would not be where I am today without the love and support of my friends, communities, and more importantly... my family.

"Since day one, they have supported my decision to join the US Army and serve my country. And since June 8, 2006 they have been with me every step of the way while I learned to live my life again.

"But this isn't another story of one Soldier's ordeal in a combat zone – this is a story about the unsung heroes, far behind the front lines, but closer to all the mental anguish it creates. I'm talking about the mothers, fathers, wives, husbands, and even the children of us Soldiers – the people who give us Soldiers the hope, motivation, and drive to do what we do... fight. I didn't join for the money, or for college – I joined to protect those I love the most. I fought because I wanted a safer world for them, and everyone else I love."

"Steadfast and Loyal."

"Steadfast and Loyal" – the motto of Brian's division, the 4th Infantry Division of the U.S. Army. And steadfast and loyal was the support Brian received from his mother, his father, his sister, and many others as he recovered from his devastating wounds.

We hear so many times of "two Soldiers killed, three injured", but we seldom get an insight into the degree of the many horrific injuries and the long road to recovery of these American Soldiers (and others in America's military). Roberta Quimby has given us an in depth look at the way Brian and his family (and many other wounded warriors and families) fought through and overcame the trauma and long road to recovery caused by the wounds of those fighting in Iraq and Afghanistan. Within these pages you'll see her emotions, her roller coaster ups and downs, her humor, and the story of an American patriot who stood by her Soldier son through thick and thin.

Roberta, who still lives in the small Massachusetts town where she grew up and raised her two children, never expected to write a book. Nor did she expect to see her only son lose both legs in a combat zone. Regular emails to family and friends kept them informed while serving as a form of therapy for Roberta. Written in the informal style of the internet, her email messages reflect the feelings and raw emotions she experienced on a daily basis. This book combines those email messages from the first fifteen months of her journey with Brian's recovery coupled with her later reflections as she chose to make her experiences available for others to learn from. All parents and those who support our military will identify with Roberta's story.

Roberta and Brian, and others like them, have shown that freedom is not free. A real price is paid by those who volunteer to preserve our freedoms – and their families also pay the price.

WHO IS SERGEANT BRIAN FOUNTAINE?

Sergeant Brian Fountaine is a proud American Soldier. He was 24 years old when he was wounded. He was 5 feet, 11 inches tall before the injury, with his prosthetics he stands 6 feet, 1 inch tall. He loves the outdoors, camping, extreme sports, video games, traveling, and dogs. Brian enlisted in the Army on 25 April 2001 after being denied enlistment in 2000 because of a non-existent asthma condition. He spent over a year making phone calls, writing emails and letters to statesmen, Congressmen, and Senators. He was finally heard, took and passed an asthma test, and immediately enlisted.

He did his Basic Combat Training and Advanced Individual Training at Fort Knox, Kentucky. Upon completion of training, he was assigned to Bravo Company, 1st Battalion, 66th Armor Regiment, 1st Brigade Combat Team, of the 4th Infantry Division at Fort Hood, Texas. He deployed with the unit to Iraq in late March 2003 and spent the next year, Operation Iraqi Freedom I, serving with the Scout platoon in Headquarters and Headquarters Company of 1st Battalion, 66th Armor Regiment. Almost nightly, he was on missions with the Scout platoon working around the area of Samarra, Iraq. Although he was not on the mission, it was Brian's brigade who captured Saddam Hussein.

Upon his return from Iraq in late March 2004, Brian began training for his second deployment to Iraq. With the reorganization of his battalion, he was transferred to Charlie Company of the same battalion where he was promoted to Sergeant and worked as a tank commander, the job he held when he was wounded on June 8, 2006 outside Taji, Iraq, northwest of Baghdad. Currently he is assigned to the Medical Hold detachment of Charlie Company pending his medical retirement from the Army, currently scheduled for October 2007.

Brian with President Bush and Roberta Quimby,
his mother – the author of this book.

Brian – High School Graduation – 2000

WHO IS SERGEANT BRIAN FOUNTAINE?

Like all other American Soldiers and Non-Commissioned Officers, Brian proudly lives by the Soldier's Creed and the NCO Creed:

THE SOLDIER'S CREED / WARRIOR ETHOS / WARRIOR CREED

I am an American Soldier.

I am a Warrior and a member of a team. I serve the people of the United States and live the Army Values.

I will always place the mission first.

I will never accept defeat.

I will never quit.

I will never leave a fallen comrade.

I am disciplined, physically and mentally tough, trained and proficient in my warrior tasks and drills. I always maintain my arms, my equipment and myself.

I am an expert and I am a professional.

I stand ready to deploy, engage, and destroy the enemies of the United States of America in close combat.

I am a guardian of freedom and the American way of life.

I am an American Soldier.

NCO CREED

No one is more professional than I. I am a Noncommissioned Officer, a leader of Soldiers. As a Noncommissioned Officer, I realize that I am a member of a time honored corps, which is known as "The Backbone of the Army". I am proud of the Corps of Noncommissioned Officers and will at all times conduct myself so as to bring credit upon the Corps, the Military Service and my country regardless of the situation in which I find myself. I will not use my grade or position to attain pleasure, profit, or personal safety.

Competence is my watchword. My two basic responsibilities will always be uppermost in my mind -- accomplishment of my mission and the welfare of my Soldiers. I will strive to remain tactically and technically proficient. I am aware of my role as a Noncommissioned Officer. I will fulfill my responsibilities inherent in that role. All Soldiers are entitled to outstanding leadership; I will provide that leadership. I know my Soldiers and I will always place their needs above my own. I will communicate consistently with my Soldiers and never leave them uninformed. I will be fair and impartial when recommending both rewards and punishment.

Officers of my unit will have maximum time to accomplish their duties; they will not have to accomplish mine. I will earn their respect and confidence as well as that of my Soldiers. I will be loyal to those with whom I serve; seniors, peers, and subordinates alike. I will exercise initiative by taking appropriate action in the absence of orders. I will not compromise my integrity, nor my moral courage. I will not forget, nor will I allow my comrades to forget that we are professionals, Noncommissioned Officers, leaders!

WHO IS SERGEANT BRIAN FOUNTAINE?

MY SON IS ALIVE...

THE PHONE CALL

It all started with a phone call on my cell phone while I was at work. I remember I was joking with fellow co-workers, laughing and just enjoying the day at work. Then my cell phone rang. The man identified himself as Captain somebody or other, rear detachment, 4th Infantry Division (4ID). My heart stopped beating for a second. But then I realized that Brian was alive. If he had been killed, they would have sent someone to tell me. When a Soldier gets injured, you just get a phone call. An awful phone call. He said that he wanted to tell me that Brian was OK. I replied back to him, that he couldn't be OK or he would not be calling me right now. "What happened to him?" And the answer would forever change my life. He told me that my son suffered a bi-lateral amputation, just below his knees. He went on to tell me how it had happened, although lots of details were missing from his story. He told me lots of things. That Brian would be transferred to Germany as soon as he was stable. He told me things that I cannot remember...

All the while, I kept having this thought that this is the part where the mother collapses to the floor and dissolves into tears. I sat down on my chair... I stood up... I sat again... And I paced the floor in front of my desk. I was crying... Tears were streaming down my face. I asked the Captain to repeat what had happened to Brian. I kept apologizing to him. I could not grasp what he was telling me. And then I asked him what bi-lateral amputation meant. That's when he said that he lost both his feet and legs, just below his knees. He lost his feet?? What do you mean he lost his feet? How can you lose your feet? How can this be happening? I remember that I started moaning. I wanted to scream, but would not do it when I was in a public place like work. I remember my co-workers leaving the office with questioning looks on their faces...

His feet are gone. I kept saying that to myself. Picturing horrible things in my mind. I still picture horrible images in my mind. Even now, six months later, I still cry thinking about it. I have to stop now. I don't want to fall apart. Not now.

My immediate supervisor came in to my office and gave me a hug. I told her what happened and she insisted that I use her office (it was private) to make any calls I needed to make. I made my way upstairs to her office, but stopped several times along the way to tell people what had happened. Most already knew, and they all wanted to give me a hug. When I got to the office, I called my husband first. It was difficult to get the words out. We did not talk long. It was hard to say anything. I wanted to call my daughter, but my ex husband had already done that. I did not realize that they would call both of us. Cassie called me and was crying. It was especially difficult for her because she was in New York with her daughter Haley. Haley's father is from New York and they were there visiting with him for a while. Cassie made arrangements to come home the next day. We were not sure who would be able to go or even where we would go. It would be either Germany or Washington DC. It was all dependent on Brian and how soon he would be transferred to Germany. He was in a hospital in Baghdad.

I walked around work aimlessly. I couldn't think. People offered to drive me home, but I didn't want to be any trouble. Like a fool, I took some work home with me. I thought I would need to work to keep busy, but that of course, did not happen. I couldn't focus or concentrate on anything. While driving home, I called my sister Robin. It was not a smart thing to do, considering I was already distracted, but I wanted to talk with her. She always had a special place in her heart for Brian, and I wanted to tell her myself. I also knew that I could count on her to make calls to the rest of the family. When she answered her cell, I asked her where she was. She told me that she was in her car, and I told her to pull over. She did, and then I told her. I don't remember what or how I told her, but I remember that she broke down. She still feels bad about it to this day, because she thought she needed to be strong for me. She has been a rock for me. How could she not break down?

Before I got home, I decided to stop by my best friend's house. Ellen is Brian's godmother and I wanted to let her know what had happened to him. I broke down while telling her. It was difficult to get the words out. Brian lost both his feet. Brian's feet were blown off by an IED (Improvised Explosive Device). It was strange, weird... I was trying to think of a way to say it so as to not shock Ellen too much, but then I realized that would be impossible. She held me and we cried together. She was trying to be strong for me. She asked if I wanted tea, and I told her sort of jokingly that a drink would be better. So she made me a drink. Just one though, because I still had to drive home.

There wasn't anyone home when I got there. I can't really remember what I did. I tried to do some work, but I couldn't focus. I paced through the house. I stared at Brian's picture hanging on the wall in the computer room. It was a warm day and the windows were open. I tell you this because of what I did next. I sat down at the computer and began really crying. You know, sobbing so hard and so much you almost choke or gag. And then for some reason, I started to scream. I screamed so loud it hurt my throat. And I still kept on screaming. I must have screamed for at least 30 to 40 seconds. I screamed until I couldn't any more. To this day, with all the business activity next door, I wonder why nobody called the police. I could have been getting murdered for God's sake.

The first email that I sent out was to Bob Babcock. He is the historian for the 4th Infantry Division. Brian's division. When Brian was deployed the first time to Iraq (in 2003-2004), I found Bob on the computer. I don't remember how, but I will always be grateful that I did find him. He did updates several times a week on the computer about what was going on with the 4ID while they were in Iraq. He reported on what he could, given the level of security, and gave family and loved ones a lot of information about how to survive while their spouses, or sons or daughters were deployed. I wanted him to know what happened to Brian, so I sent him an email. I will always remember how he gave me support and strength through the days and weeks to come.

I spent the rest of the day waiting for more phone calls. I remember vaguely that I received several calls from different people in the Army. Most of them were part of the rear detachment for the 4ID. Paul (my ex) and I were advised to get the process started for passports. We were told that we would probably be flown to Germany at a moment's notice, so we could be with Brian. That never happened though, and I am grateful for that. A long flight to Germany would have been very difficult on all of us. I'm pretty sure we were told a lot of things, but I could not remember much of anything.

So begins my journey to hell and back. This has been the most exhausting and difficult thing that I have ever done or gone through. Or experienced

My email updates were a way to stay in touch with family and friends. They were a way to feel normal for a little while. They were the contact with what I was familiar with.

When I say journey to hell and back, I don't necessarily mean just for me. Watching and witnessing what Brian went through and what he continues to go through has been hell. For him. For me. For his father, Paul. For his sister, Cassie. It continues to be hell. There are moments of great joy and hope, and moments of total despair. The good moments are beginning to outweigh the bad. That is progress – a "step" in the right direction.

Thursday, 8 Jun 2006 11:24

Dear Mr. Babcock,

I don't know why, but I feel the need to tell you about my son. His name is Sgt. Brian Fountaine and he is with the 4th Infantry Division, 1-66 Armor, in Iraq. He was injured this morning. I got a phone call from a Captain Hanson from Fort Hood. He was in a Humvee, which I don't know why as he is a tank commander, and they hit an IED. Brian had to have a bilateral amputation. His right leg from the knee down and his left from the ankle down. I can't even begin to express how I feel at the moment. I feel as though I am losing my mind. My son, my first born... He has no feet... This happened to him – why?? I can't seem to remember now...

I'm sorry to burden you with this but I had to do something, I had to tell someone.

Roberta Quimby

This next email was sent to friends and family members on my husband's side. I knew I did not have the strength to call them all.

Thu, 8 Jun 2006 11:48

Hi Everyone,

       I'm sorry that I am telling you all this way, but this is the easiest way for me. I got a call this morning from the Army. Brian was seriously injured by an IED this morning, Baghdad time. He is going to be ok, but lost his right leg just below the knee and his left foot at the ankle. He is in recovery now, and will be transferred to Germany as soon as he is able. His father and I will be going to Germany to be with him. We don't know when, but the Army will arrange everything.

       That's really all I know right now. Please keep him in your prayers. He is going to need them.

Roberta

From here on in, the emails I sent out were to immediate family and friends. I still called some, but it was so much easier to keep everyone informed by email. I would never have been able to get through all the phone calls. My contact list got bigger and bigger as time went by. Everyone wanted to know how Brian was doing.

Picture of Brian that hangs in Roberta's computer room

THE AGONY OF WAITING

Sat, 10 Jun 2006 03:36

Hi everyone,

No call over night, and I did manage to get some sleep. The last call I got last night I was told that Brian is in critical but stable condition. He has developed some fluid in his lungs, so the need to watch and deal with that. I haven't heard if they moved him to Germany, but I suspect they will wait until that situation is dealt with. So I really don't know anything more.

I thank you all for your prayers, and please keep them coming. I somehow can feel them.

I won't be leaving the house till I hear from Brian. If I missed his call I don't think I could take that. So I'm just gonna hang here and try to do some work.

I will keep you all posted when I hear anything today, either by email or phone.

Love,
Roberta

I was in agony waiting for some news of Brian. I could think of nothing else. I kept picturing in my mind what the explosion was like. I wanted to know how it happened. Why was he in a Humvee and not his tank? We got lots of calls from different Army personnel, but they didn't have any concrete information on Brian. They knew just what we knew. It was frustrating.

My mind also replayed memories of Brian as a youngster – before he joined the Army. Lots of memories – some big, some small…

Brian has always enjoyed building and creating. When he was very young, we got him his first Lego set and he is still buying them to this day. He built the most amazing vehicles and buildings, and cities. He also loves to draw and is quite good at it. He always took art classes in high school and excelled at them.

For as long as I can remember, playing Army was his favorite thing to do. He had all the "gear" that an 11 year old could come up with, and made up some of his own. He spent hours in the woods, building forts and playing war games with his friends. He built a zip line from a big pine tree to the shed in our back yard. I remember one day getting a knock on the door and seeing a fireman standing there. He said they had a report of a fire in the woods, and kids lighting it. Come to find out, Brian and a friend built a campfire in the woods and had taken some hot dogs from home to roast on the fire. After the firemen put the campfire out they told me that Brian had built the perfect, safest campfire they had ever seen. Brian was a member of the Boy Scouts up until about the 7th grade. He loved the projects they did and especially loved the Pinewood Derby.

He played town sports all his childhood. He tried soccer for a couple of years and football as well, but his love was baseball. His dad, Paul, a Boston Firefighter, coached some of the teams that he played on. He also played basketball and scored the winning three pointer from half court during a playoff game. There was barely any time left on the clock and the audience was screaming for him to just shoot, so he did – from half court, and guess what??? Nothing but Net!!! Swish... That was an amazing moment with everyone surrounding him and slapping him on the back. He was not a standout in basketball, so this was all the more special.

He played high school football and baseball. He was a good student, but I had to prod him to read and do his homework. He always had a part time job – from paper routes to working at the local hardware store and restaurants. He was not afraid to work. He liked earning his own money.

And yes, video games... from the first ones that ever came out, to the latest newest up to date games, he has always loved playing. He likes competition and he likes the planning and plotting that is involved in some of the games.

Brian knew before he graduated that he wanted to serve his country. He graduated from high school in 2000 and immediately began his pursuit to join the military. I never knew pain until the day he left for basic training. He was dating Emily. They seemed to be serious, but it did not last too long. Emily made the trip to Fort Knox with Cassie and me to see him graduate, but they soon parted ways. Anyway, the day that he left, he had been staying at Emily's house so the three of us went to lunch. He had to report to the recruiter's office at 2:00 pm. We went to a Chinese restaurant for lunch and I remember how hard it seemed to be. I had never had to say goodbye to my son, and I did not know how I would be. I soon found out.

I remember standing in the driveway at Emily's parent's house, and just wishing this was not happening. As I think about that moment, I can still feel the gut wrenching pain that came over me the minute I hugged him and said goodbye. I cried all the way home and was a bit afraid that I would crash my car because my vision was blurry.

The weirdest thing happened though. When I pulled into my driveway, my husband, Chet, who is a local truck driver, was there with his tractor trailer. He was driving by the house, and decided to stop, but he was not sure why. When I got out of the car, he walked up to me, and just put his arms around me and held me tight. I sobbed. I can still remember that pain of letting Brian go. Of not knowing what was going to happen to him in basic training and how he was going to handle it – and maybe dreading that the reality of what I'm dealing with now would happen. If Chet had not been there, I'm not sure what I would have done.

My thoughts came back to the present time… I also wondered how it must be to have the job to call family and give them the news that their son or daughter or husband or wife was seriously injured. Obviously, knocking on someone's door to tell them their loved one had died would be worse. I was always afraid some day I would see a vehicle with government plates on it pull up in the driveway. I will be forever grateful that Brian is alive. He will never go back there again.

Sat, 10 Jun 2006 10:22

Hi everyone,

I spoke with Brian's nurse this morning. She told me that Brian has made some vast improvements in the last couple of hours. His oxygen level is much better now, but they are going to keep him on the respirator until they get him to Germany, just as a precaution. They said he was in good spirits and she told me that he was a very brave young man. He has a small cut on his face and no other injuries except to his legs. She told me that they are taking very good care of him, and he should be leaving Iraq for Germany in the next few hours. They still are hoping to keep him in Germany for just a couple of days at the most, as they want to get him to Walter Reed in Washington, DC as soon as they can. It will be easier for us to go to Washington than to Germany, but we will just wait and see. I'm anxious to speak to him, to hear his voice, but with the respirator that's not going to happen for a while.

This is all I know for now. Thank you all for your thoughts and prayers, and keep them coming!

Love,
Roberta

I burst into tears the moment I got off the phone with his nurse. I wish I could remember her name. She was very kind, and told me all the things I needed to hear. But I wanted to be by his side. I physically ached to put my hand on his forehead, or hold his hand in mine. I was crazy with the need to do something and yet I was paralyzed to do anything. It was the strangest feeling. I paced the house from room to room. I would try to do some housework, but couldn't. I thought I was losing my mind, and actually felt that would be better than being so sick with worry.

Sun, 11 Jun 2006 07:02

Hi everyone,

I hadn't heard anything in such a long time so I called his nurse in Iraq. Brian is in Germany now, and just before I talked to his nurse in Iraq, she got a call telling her that he is off the ventilator and doing well. That is good news. I'm hoping to hear from him today, and if not, his nurse in Germany. Maybe by the end of the day we will know when or how soon he will be back in the States.

That's it for now. Thanks for your thoughts and prayers.

Love,
Roberta

It took a few phone calls to get the number for his nurse in Iraq. It is really weird dialing phone numbers in other countries. I was glad that I did though, because I needed some news about Brian. I really needed to talk to him and hear his voice, but I settled for what information I got from his nurse.

People started dropping by the house by this time – some women from the Military Support Group, and some men from the American Legion here in Hanson, Massachusetts. They offered hugs and prayers, some vital information, and calling cards. We even received a beautiful fruit basket, which was a good thing, because I was incapable of cooking. I was pretty much incapable of anything at that point. I could not focus or concentrate. I could not finish any type of task – like housework, bill paying, or even laundry.

Sun 11 Jun 2006 19:16

Hi all,

I'm not sure who I emailed or spoke to today. It's just a big blur. I spoke to Brian this morning and he also spoke with Paul, his dad. He sounded tired and his voice was strained from the ventilator, but that is normal. He told me that it was his fault, that he didn't see the IED that exploded. He was pretty good at spotting them. His father filled me in on some things also. Brian's gunner on the Humvee was killed and the driver lost a leg. Brian applied a tourniquet to himself and then to the driver, and basically saved their lives. They are telling us what a brave man he is.

I just called the nurse who is taking care of him. She said he is in considerable pain, having a burning sensation in his legs. They have him on an epidural with two pain meds to keep him comfortable. He is having trouble sleeping also – flashbacks starting already. Hopefully they will get him help for that ASAP (as soon as possible). He is scheduled for surgery in the morning for a "wash out", which is just as it implies. If all goes well, he will fly to Washington to Walter Reed Hospital on Tuesday. I plan on being there when he gets there – one way or the other. The Army is supposed to take care of transportation and a place to stay. Paul, Cassie, and I and possibly Haley (our granddaughter), will be going.

That's about all I know right now. I'm worn out and going to try to sleep. Thank you all for your kind words and prayers. Keep them coming.

Love,
Roberta

That call to Brian was definitely the hardest phone call I had ever had. I was so happy to hear his voice. I knew that he was alive, and that he would survive this, but I so badly needed to hear his voice. I did not want to cry, and it was a struggle not to. I kept saying his name over and over again. I kept telling him that he was going to be ok and that he was alive. I don't even know if he heard me.

The next words that came from him sent a chill up my spine and nearly broke my heart. "They got me Mom, they got me". "I know they did, those bastards," was my reply.

And then the words came out of his mouth – the words that would haunt me, and him, for a long time to come. The words that I somehow knew would come from his mouth. "It was my fault, Mom. My fault". Of course I asked him what he meant by that, and how it could possibly be his fault. He said it was his fault, because he was the one who made the decision to go in the direction that they traveled.

At the time, I was under the mistaken assumption that his gunner was killed and the driver badly injured. I don't know how that misinformation was told to Paul and to me. It's entirely possible that in our shock we misunderstood what was told to us.

You cannot imagine how many phone calls we received from Army personnel. Add to those calls, family, friends, people from the local military support group, members of Legion Posts, the town's Veterans Agent. There was no end to them. They all had advice to offer, and information to give.

Anyway, his gunner was not killed. He actually survived the blast with no injuries at all. His driver did lose a leg in the blast. Brian lost both legs.

I knew from the tone of Brian's voice, that it would be useless to argue the point with him. I did not want to upset him any more than he already was. So I told him that I was so glad that he was alive, and that I did not know what I would do if he did not survive this. I told him how badly I wanted to see him, and how much I loved him. I also told him that I was very proud of him. For serving his country. For doing his duty. I still am proud of him. He is a hero to me, although he certainly doesn't think so. Not then and not now. I told him we would meet him in Washington as soon as they gave us the go ahead.

Already, he was dealing with phantom pain. A term that we would become very familiar with over the next several months. I didn't know what exactly it meant, but I knew he was hurting because of it. A few weeks later he was able to describe to me what the pain was like. He was struggling to understand what was happening to him and what had happened to him. To his body, and to his soul.

At this point, because we were not sure if he would be staying in Germany or would be transferred to Walter Reed, I went to the Town Hall in Hanson, my home town, to inquire about passports. When I got there, I asked the clerk how to go about getting a passport. She told me that I would have to go to Whitman, the next town over, and apply there. I broke down at that point, and began crying. I told her that my son was severely wounded in Iraq and that I may need to fly to Germany at a moment's notice. I wanted someone else to feel my pain. I wanted the world to know what had happened to my son.

I drove to the Town Hall in Whitman and pretty much did the same thing. I could not get the words out of my mouth without breaking down. The woman there was very helpful and assured me that she would push the passports through. I had to get Cassie's and my birth certificates and bring them back.

I cannot describe the feeling that I had as I walked through the building. I wanted to shout and scream. I was angry and completely devastated. I wanted to see Brian and be with Brian. I didn't care where or how, I just needed to see him. To hold his hand. To rub his head. To make his pain go away.

I spent Monday just trying to get organized and packed. I wanted to be ready for whatever the Army was going to tell us. They had let us know that we needed to be ready at a moment's notice to fly to wherever. The plan was for him to come to Walter Reed within the next 24 hours, depending on how he was responding. All we could do was wait. And that was so hard. I was sure I would lose my mind. You can not imagine the things that were going through my head. I was so afraid that something would happen to him medically and he would not survive the trauma of what had happened. I was so afraid I would never see him again.

People kept stopping by the house. They wanted to drop off cards to bring to Brian. They wanted to just give me a hug and let me know they were praying for us. Some of these people had sons who were in Iraq, or who had been in Iraq. They knew what I was going through, and I imagine it frightened them to think that this may happen to their son or daughter.

Brian in his tank in Iraq – January 2006
He was in a Humvee, not this tank, when wounded.

Purple Heart earned by Brian. The Purple Heart has been awarded
since the Revolutionary War to those wounded in action.

MY SON IS ALIVE...

BRIAN ARRIVES AT WALTER REED

Tues, 13 Jun 2006 16:48

Hi everyone,

Just a quick update. Brian arrived a little while ago at Walter Reed in Washington. I was able to talk to him for a few minutes. He is in a lot of pain and exhausted, but otherwise ok. He will be evaluated and that process takes several hours. When it is determined that Walter Reed is the best place for him, the Army will call us and tell us our flight information. Pray that they keep him at Walter Reed. The other option is a hospital in Texas. We are all packed and ready to go, just waiting for the word.

I will try to keep you updated as much as possible. Please keep the prayers coming.

Love,
Roberta

I was so relieved that he was back in the States. Although I would have flown to Germany in a second, I did not relish the thought of flying there. It would have been very exhausting. We could do nothing except wait for a call. It was frustrating. I wanted to be there and to know what was going on and what they were doing to him. I really could not stand it, the not knowing.

I kept telling myself that I would move mountains to keep him in Washington. Brian told me he wanted to stay there and did not under any circumstances want to go to Texas. He hates Texas, too many bad memories for him there. He was stationed at Fort Hood in Texas, and met, married, and divorced a girl who never really loved him. I'm not sure what she was all about, and I guess I never will know. But Texas was out of the question.

Tues, 13 Jun 2006 20:37

Hi all,

Just wanted to share with you. Brian called around 10:15. He sounded so much better. Obviously the pain meds were given and they helped. He sounded like his old self, even joked about his "sponge bath" that he received. He is anxious for us to be there for him, as am I. Thank you for your prayers. Keep them coming.

Love,
Roberta

How I kidded myself. How I made myself believe that Brian was still Brian. That he would be ok. That he would be the same young man who left for the Army to fulfill a life long dream. He always wanted to be in the military, for as long as I could remember. He actually wanted to join the Air Force. But they rejected him for medical reasons. They said he had asthma. Something he did not have. When he was 12 or 13, he had bronchitis, and it was stubborn in responding to antibiotics. His doctor gave him an inhaler to help with his breathing and that was the only time he ever used it. But according to the Air Force, that made him an asthmatic. The Army took him though.

The day I said good bye to him when he left for boot camp was the second most difficult day in my life. I never felt such pain before. It was so hard to say good bye to him. Knowing that I would not know where he was and what he was doing any more. His life was out of my hands. He belonged to the United States of America.

How I worried when he was in boot camp. But when we went to his graduation, I was surprised at the man he had become. He was no longer a child. He was a Soldier of the United States Army. He was a man, and I was so proud of him and who he had become.

Wed, 14 Jun 2006 05:12

Hi Everyone,

We are leaving at 1:30 this afternoon and will be in Washington by 3:15. He is staying at Walter Reed. Thank God.

His address is:

Sgt. Brian Fountaine
Walter Reed Army Medical Center …

I will keep you posted as much as possible while we are there. Thank you all again for your prayers.

Love,
Roberta

I will never forget that address. It is burned into my memory. After a week, I could recite it by heart. And I did – many, many times.

So now we fly to DC. Cassie, Haley, Paul, and myself. Yes, traveling with my ex-husband. That was interesting, to say the least. We actually get along pretty well, but it felt awkward. When Brian had to leave for the first time for boot camp, he wanted to have a dinner with just the four of us. It was the first time that we had done that since the divorce, and although I was a nervous wreck, it went pretty well. I tried to think of it as having dinner with a long lost relative. I asked him about his family and he asked me about mine, it was weird. And since that time, we have had many dinners together with the kids and with our significant others as well. It always works out ok.

But traveling to DC – I had no idea if we were going to have our own rooms or not. The Army made all the arrangements and they were aware that we were divorced. I let them know that it would not be a problem traveling together, but nothing was ever said about a hotel room. All I can say about the flight was thank God for Haley. She was a trooper and was her usual charming self. She was and is a happy baby, a beautiful baby, who could make you smile with just one look. Cassie and Haley were the buffers between Paul and me, but I'm not sure if it was necessary. We were both anxious and worried and did not know what to expect. We both knew that Brian needed us, and he needed us to be united. And that is what we were. United for him. United because of him.

The Army did a good job with the travel arrangements. We were picked up at Reagan Airport by a limo and driven straight to the Mologne House. That is a hotel right on the property of Walter Reed Army Medical Hospital. Walter Reed is just like any other Army base, complete with its own police and fire departments. It is definitely a world within itself. Once there, we registered and found out that we would be sharing a room. I really did not care, because it was quite clear from the activity in the lobby of the Mologne House that it was a very busy place. I was grateful that we had a room there. Some families were forced to stay at hotels in and around the DC area. That meant finding ways back and forth to the hospital, and it just made things more difficult.

Wed, 14 Jun 2006 20:41

Hi All,

We finally got to see Brian around 6:00 pm. He had surgery around noon and was in recovery until then. He is doing amazingly well considering... He is in a lot of pain, and having trouble with keeping it under control, but the anesthesiologist came by around an hour ago, and increased the dose he was getting in his epidural. His mood goes from very happy to be alive, to angry and blaming himself for what happened. He told us what happened and before I pass that on, I want to make sure it is ok with him. I did find out that no one died. It was only Brian and his driver, Specialist Jones, who were injured. Jones lost a leg in the explosion and was sent to San Antonio, Texas. I think that is nearer to his home. I'm not sure how that misinformation came about. Things are a blur.

Brian's Dad is spending the night in his hospital room with him, and I think we are going to take turns doing that. He can't sleep well, and I think it helps if one of us is there. He is already talking about the future and I think that is a very good sign. I'm very hopeful and very encouraged.

I am also completely exhausted, so I am going to get some rest now. It has been a long, emotional day. Cassie and Haley are fast asleep. Haley is the most awesome baby. She was a trooper all day today. What a blessing. Keep the prayers coming.

Love,
Roberta

As soon as we dropped our bags off in the room we wanted to get over to the hospital. Of course we had no idea how to get there from the Mologne House. We inquired at the desk and they told us we could wait for the shuttle bus which comes every half hour or we could walk. We chose to walk and they gave us directions. It was then, during our walk over to the hospital, that we realized we were in a whole new world. We saw more amputees on that first walk over than I had seen in my whole life. They were all sizes and shapes and colors. Legs, arms, an arm and leg, both legs. It was an amazing sight. I remember watching them all just going about their business, and feeling such a wave of hope and optimism. It was June and very warm in DC. Most of the amputees were wearing shorts. They were proud of their new legs and arms. If they had been wearing pants, you would not have known they were amputees. I wondered how Brian would look when he was able to walk. I wondered how long it would take him to get to the point that some of these men and women were – walking normally.

I could not wait to see Brian, but at the same time I was afraid. I didn't know what to expect and what he would look like. I was actually afraid that I would be repulsed by his legs – that I would not be able to look at them, what was left of them. I didn't know. And I was a little afraid to find out.

As time went on, I was astonished at how quickly I became "comfortable" with his legs. When his bandages were removed, I was right there wanting to see what they looked like. My "mother" instincts kicked in and I wanted to see what had happened to my son's body. I wanted to examine his whole body and see what his injuries were. I didn't of course. He would have killed me!!

Brian was in Ward 45C, just a step down from intensive care. We walked into his room and I remember his eyes were shut. I went next to his bed and leaned over and said his name. He opened his eyes and smiled a little and said, "Hi, Mom."

Like a big baby, I just started crying. I put my arms around him as best I could. His legs were elevated, and covered with thick bandages. I remember glancing at them briefly, but wanted only to look into his eyes and see for myself that he was going to be ok. I saw pain, confusion, guilt, and anger. But I saw my son. My smiling friend. My Brian. He needed me, and I could not fall apart. As much as I wanted to, I had to be strong for him. We both cried. He told me that he loved me, and that he was glad we were there. I told him he was going to be ok. He was going to survive this. I told him I loved him. He told me it was his fault. This is where I almost lost it. He was going to blame himself for this. I somehow knew that he would feel responsible for what had happened.

While Paul stayed with Brian that first night, I went back to the hotel to try and sleep. It was difficult, but I did manage to get some rest. The next morning, I went back to the hospital to relieve Paul and be with Brian. Cass and Haley came with me. We were not supposed to allow Haley into his room, because of the bacteria that all Soldiers bring back from Iraq. They all have it and get treated with antibiotics to kill it. We had to wash our hands and use the anti-bacterial sanitizers for your hands when we came in and out of his room. We decided to "sneak" Haley into his room anyway. He had not seen her, and we felt it would be good for him to meet his niece. I'm glad that we did because when we came into his room with her, he said hello to her and she gave him the biggest smile back. Her face lit up, and his did in return. It was funny, like she knew that he needed her beautiful smile. And boy, did she give him one.

They didn't stay in the room too long though, because of the restrictions. I stayed with Brian and just held his hand and rubbed his head. I used to rub his head when he was younger. He had awful headaches sometimes, and it seemed to help when I massaged his head.

He started to look as though he was in pain. I spoke to his nurse, and she told me that she had put a call in to the anesthesiologists to come and either increase the dosage of medicine going into his epidural or change it. I gave it a while and they had not come, so I spoke to her again. I let her know that he was in pain and it was getting worse. Still they did not come.

That was when I had my "Shirley McClaine, Terms of Endearment" moment. I went to the nurses' station, and began yelling that my son was in pain. I yelled that after all he had gone through and all he lost he should not have to suffer with pain. I was crying and yelling at the same time. It was actually the best thing though, because within a couple of minutes the doctors were there, assessing Brian, and talking about what they could do for his pain. I felt a little funny about my little meltdown, but also realized that was probably the only way to get them to come. They don't really like hysterical parents at hospitals.

I can't remember what they ended up giving him for his pain. He had tried so many drugs in the beginning to help. Whatever they gave him, it helped a lot and he began to feel more comfortable. He also began to talk and to tell me what had happened. I was very afraid to hear what he had to say, but at the same time, I could not stop myself from listening.

Brian is a tank commander. He should have been in a tank, not a humvee. Actually they called it an up-armored humvee. Notice the past tense. So much for up-armored. Anyway, Brian's lieutenant asked for volunteers to take the humvee and test a device that was supposed to block signals to IEDs. This would prevent them from exploding when they were signaled to by someone.

Brian was supposed to patrol the area with his driver and a gunner trying to disrupt signals. They came to a fork in the road, and were not sure which direction to go. Brian made the decision – that was his job, what he was trained to do. Brian remembers flying up in the air, and then he remembers lying face down in the sand, in a hole. He rolled over and looked at his legs and knew right away that he was badly hurt. His driver was screaming. His gunner appeared to be in shock.

Brian knew that he had to get control of the situation or there would be more casualties to talk about on the evening news. He ordered his gunner to help him by getting some tourniquets. The gunner searched for them, but in the meantime, Brian took his belt off and applied a tourniquet to his leg. He needed one for his other leg also, and he knew that the driver needed one applied to his leg as well. The gunner finally came through with a tourniquet for Brian to use on his other leg.

He instructed the young gunner, who had only been with Brian's unit for a short time, on what to do. Brian remained calm, and basically saved his own life and the life of his driver. Help arrived and took over the situation.

They were medivaced to the hospital in Baghdad, where Brian's legs were amputated. They had to cleanly cut each leg so he would be able to heal. At the same time, his lung collapsed and they had to intubate him. The hospital in Baghdad did an excellent job keeping him alive. In an earlier war, he would have had little chance of surviving this type of injury.

I have listened to Brian tell the story of what happened to him a couple of times. It is, and will always be, very hard for me to listen to. I cannot do it without crying. It doesn't get easier to hear each time either. It breaks my heart to hear what he went through. It breaks my heart to hear him talk about his time in Iraq – what he went through and what he saw.

I am enormously proud of him and what he was doing in Iraq. I know what his intentions were, and I know he cared for the people there, at least the people who wanted to be helped, the ones who wanted their freedom. It was a difficult mission for him and for a lot of Soldiers. But it was a mission that he took seriously, and a mission that he intended to accomplish. He never questioned his mission. He never wavered.

He was eventually medivaced to Germany where they kept him for barely 24 hours. They wanted to make sure he was stable for the flight to Washington. There were so many Soldiers arriving in Washington. So many casualties. So many deaths. I would see first hand the damage the enemy was doing to our men and women. The damage they continue to do.

BRIAN ARRIVES AT WALTER REED

Fri, 16 Jun 2006 11:29

Hi everyone,

Good news to report today. Brian is doing so much better. He was moved to another ward, Ward 57, but he has his own room. They still call them wards, but they are all private rooms. He sat up in a wheelchair today, and some really amazing things happened. He got a visit from Johnny Damon and a couple of other Yankee players. They are in town this weekend to play the Nationals. The funny thing was they tried to get him to put on a Yankee hat for a photo op, and Brian flat out told them, "No way", because he is a Red Sox fan from Boston. Johnny got a kick out of that. They took pictures anyway and signed hats and stuff for him.

I also met Johnny and shook his hand and thanked him for coming to meet with the Soldiers. It was a good thing that he did, it's not easy to meet some of these guys here. There was also a young and rising female country singer who came in to meet him, but I forget her name. She was real pretty, and Brian said he was going to start listening to country if all the female singers were this cute, LOL (email code for "laugh out loud").

His spirits are good. He has another wash out tomorrow to clean the stumps and will have another cut down on Tuesday to even them off. He has a severe fracture in the lower half of the left leg that they will remove when they do the cut down. That will be good because it's causing him a lot of pain, more so than the other leg. His lung collapsed in Baghdad and he still has the chest tube in, but hopefully that should come out later today or tomorrow.

I'm going to go rest because I'm staying at the hospital with him tonight. There's a recliner in the room, and he has three quilts from people who make them and donate them to the Soldiers. They are beautiful.

The prayers are helping, I believe. Keep them coming.

Love,
Roberta

MY SON IS ALIVE...

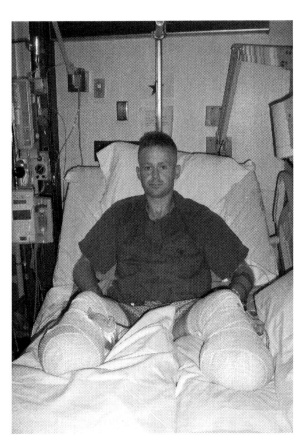

Brian's first day at Walter Reed

THE HOSPITAL ROUTINE BEGINS

I thought I was exhausted then, but I had no idea how tired I would really become. The routine in the hospital would establish itself quickly, and I did more running around than I thought I could endure. At times, I would just stop and sit on one of the benches in the hallways, or go outside and sit out there just to rest for a few minutes. When I was in Brian's room, I could not sit. I was always doing something. I tried to organize the cards that had already started coming in. He received care packages from the Red Cross and other organizations, and all of that had to be put somewhere. The hospital rooms were very small and the lockers were a joke.

I was also nursing him at the same time. Not that the nurses at Walter Reed were not doing their job, because most of them were excellent. But there were just so many patients and they had their hands full. I wanted to do whatever I could for him. I emptied urinals and commodes, refreshed his water pitcher, got him some Boost drinks, a nutritious drink to supplement his diet. His wounds and the trauma left his body weak and deprived of vitamins and nutrients.

I rubbed his head a lot. He had a lot of headaches. I even helped to change his bandages. The one thing that bothered me the most was the wound vac machine. He had a tube attached to each stump that connected to the machine, and the machine would literally "vac" the wound to help keep it clean. Between the noise it made, and being able to see what was vac'd from his leg, I grew to hate that machine and we all rejoiced when they finally removed it.

I also helped him transfer from bed to wheelchair and he enjoyed "prowling" the halls of the hospital. There were plenty of them. Sometimes we would go outside and just "walk" a bit, actually I walked and pushed his wheelchair. He would make phone calls then because the reception was horrible inside the hospital.

We went to the cafeteria one day and had lunch there instead of in his room. He said the food in the cafeteria made him sick so he refused to eat there again. I ate there for breakfast and lunch just about every day during the week. There was a Subway, but I don't care what that Jared guy says in the commercial, you can get very fat eating there on a regular basis! LOL! The cafeteria became a familiar place and a comfort zone for me. I felt safe there and was able to relax for a while. I began to become familiar with other families and with staff and felt a kinship to some of them.

There was always something to do. I was not used to keeping up this pace and it knocked me for a loop. And none of what I just said had anything to do with the enormous amount of paperwork that Brian began to receive from the Army, the VA, and the hospital. It was overwhelming, and continued to be overwhelming. I have never seen anything like it. The red tape, the forms, it all became too much at times. Just thinking about it now gives me a headache.

My company stepped up to the plate big time for Brian and me. I kept in touch with them through Yahoo instant messages and they were always asking what Brian or I needed. I had heard through the hospital grapevine that laptops were a coveted item at the hospital and a wonderful morale booster for the patients. When Brian was in Iraq, the computer was his lifeline to home, family, and friends. So I told my supervisor, Julanne, that he could probably use one. She told me she would make it happen, and, by God, she did. Within two days, a laptop was delivered to Brian, and had everything installed on it that he could possibly want, including a security system that used the touch of his fingertip to access. It was pretty cool.

The other thing that they did was to continue to pay me even when I was in DC. It was pretty amazing. I had only been with them for a little over a year, and started out as a temp. At first, I thought they were being generous with vacation time, but in time I realized what they were doing, and I emailed the "big boss" in Chicago to thank him for what the company was doing. He told me that Brian sacrificed a lot to serve his country and it was the least they could do for him, and for me. I was very touched and moved by what he said to me. I still have that email saved. I have to say that what they did basically saved me from financial ruin.

The Army paid for our flights to and from DC. They also paid us to be Brian's non-medical attendants. While he was in-patient, they paid Paul, Cassie and me – I think it was $55 a day. They called it a food allowance. There is just no way you could spend $55 a day eating at the hospital cafeteria!!! Then when Brian became an outpatient, one of us would get paid while we were there with him. It certainly helped, but my company paying me while I was with Brian was huge. We also did not have to pay for the hotel we stayed at inside the Walter Reed complex. The Mologne House has about 200 rooms and is full all the time. That's another story for another chapter though.

Sat, 17 Jun 2006 11:08

Hi All,

Just a quick update. I spent the night in Brian's hospital room. He was exhausted from all the day's activities, and slept pretty good. They came for him early this morning and too him for another wash out to clean out his stumps. They took the chest tube out shortly after that and he was in a lot of pain from it. They are keeping an eye on him and doing chest x-rays to make sure his lungs are ok. He is sleeping now and we are taking a break at the hotel room. It gets pretty quiet here on the weekends. On Tuesday he has his final cut down. I'm not looking forward to that because I know he will be hurting after that, but then it's forward progress for him. They were saying that he will be fitted at least five times for his prosthesis in the first year. It's going to be a long road for him. He wavers but mostly he is strong and in good spirits.

Not sure when I'm coming home. I'm playing that by ear right now. Keep the prayers coming.

Love,
Roberta

You would not believe all the celebrities we met. Most were actually very nice and seemed very interested in the Soldier, how he got hurt, and how he was doing. They were polite, listened to them, and asked questions. Some of the politicians and the military higher ups were really just putting their time in. At least, that is how I felt. Of all people, the first one that Brian met was Johnny Damon - the ex Red Sox turned traitor, I mean Yankee. He was very nice though, and it was a good thing that he did, coming by to meet some of the Soldiers.

When there was a VIP coming through, the staff would come around and ask each patient if they wanted to meet that person. They respected your privacy if you were not interested. If you wanted to meet them, they would come in the room with a group of people. Most of them were either security or staff from the hospital, and they would take your picture with the VIP on a Polaroid so you had it and usually the VIP autographed it. We met sports figures, movie stars, and singers. Jason Alexander from Seinfeld, Nicolette Sheriden, Michael Bolton, the guy from the Sopranos, James Gandolfini, Cher, some of the guys from Aerosmith, a couple of country western singers whose names remain lost in my mind somewhere, and some movie star from the show "The OC". Bo Derek, and that cute guy from Northern Exposure who was the disc jockey. He was also on Sex in the City as one of Carrie's boyfriends. He was very cute, and I told him that I enjoyed him on Northern Exposure.

Brian had so many surgeries I lost count after a while. The first ones were pretty much "wash outs" to clean the stumps so they would heal better. This was to also help with keeping infections from his stumps. While he was in-patient we were able to wait in his room or even go back to the hotel for a while. Brian never remembered much about these surgeries. He was always surprised to wake up suddenly in recovery and ask when they were going to take him into surgery. He was impressed with the drugs he was given before surgery, they worked well! He was always groggy and sleepy after, and sometimes would wake up in the middle of the night wanting to eat, or go to the bathroom, or just talk. His father and I made sure one of us was there for him those first few weeks.

Brian wanted that chest tube out in the worst way. He wanted every tube out of him. It had come to a point where they were annoying him a lot. He would tape his IV to his arm and his chest tube to his chest. He hated it when they pulled or tugged. It hurt and was uncomfortable.

They finally took the chest tube out after he came back to his room. I wish they had taken it out while he was under the anesthesia, it hurt a lot when they removed it. I hated to see him in pain. It would almost always bring on a fresh stream of tears.

One night, one his nurses accidentally yanked on his catheter tubing. Brian told me he wanted to kill her when she did that. He wanted the catheter out, but certainly not that way. She told him she was sorry, but did not seem very sincere about it. Brian spoke to the head nurse and requested that lady not be his nurse any more. She never came back into his room after that night.

Most of his nurses were great. Some were private citizens and some were Army. There was a nurse in intensive care who took extra special care of him, at least it seemed that way to Brian and me. She even gave him her St. Christopher's necklace and told him she wanted it back when he was able to walk again. She came to visit him when he was moved to Ward 57 and he would visit her when she was on duty. They seemed to be developing a relationship and I was not sure what to make of it. Brian had gone through some rough times with the women in his life and I worried that he would be hurt. Yet at the same time, I felt like she was a boost for his morale, which at times was frightfully low.

He was mostly angry, and most of it was directed at himself. He still blamed himself for what happened. He talked to me about it in detail. He said his first instinct was to go in one direction, but then at the last minute he decided to go the other way. It was his responsibility to take care of his men, and to complete his mission. He felt like he failed on both. I think that he has since come to terms with what happened and does not blame himself so much any more. That was a result of being in Texas after his unit came back from Iraq. He talked with his men and got a much different perspective on all of it.

I knew from early on that he was going to have trouble emotionally. How could he not?? I cannot begin to imagine what he has gone through or even pretend to know how he feels. I only know what I felt. And what he told me.

Mon, 19 Jun 2006 06:07

Hi all,

I took the day off yesterday from the updates. I was exhausted and Brian had me running all over hell's creation pushing his wheelchair. They let him get in one so he wanted to go outside, to the cafeteria, and to the 4th floor to visit the nurse who was very good to him when he was in ICU, and very cute as well!! He exhausted himself pretty good and was in a lot of pain last night - phantom and real. He did manage some sleep though.

We have a meeting with the family assistance people today and should get a better idea of what to expect. There is sooo much information to absorb for all of us, it's exhausting. Brian will have PT today, and surgery tomorrow. I dread the surgery, because I know what he will be in for afterwards with the pain, and he is determined to get the epidural out and won't take any extra pain meds now. Stubborn SOB...

I discussed with him the possibility of me staying on indefinitely. He will be outpatient in a few weeks and will stay here at the Mologne House. They encourage family members to be here throughout their rehab to help. I'm talking a few months at the very least… We will have more of an idea soon, I hope. He wants me to stay with him, but he doesn't want to impose. Anyway, that will be a decision to make in a day or two. I just want to get through the surgery.

Paul, Cassie and Anthony (Haley's daddy, who drove down from New York) insisted on me going out to dinner with them last night. We went to a restaurant on the banks of the Potomac. It was very nice and I was glad that I went. Brian and Anthony get along great, as well as him and Paul, so it's kind of funny watching the three of them gang up on Cassie. She doesn't know what to make of it. Cass and Anthony have been doing a lot of running around getting things for Brian that they don't have here on base, like the remote controlled fan that he just loves. They have been a blessing.

Did I tell you about Cher?? She was here a couple of days ago and held Haley and had a picture taken holding her. It's weird here with celebrities coming and going. There was another one yesterday, some actress from a TV show…

Anyway, I have to go shower for the meeting at 10. I stayed with Brian last night in his hospital room and I'm pooped. I'm looking forward to a nice nap later. It's very hot here, just like back home. I'm rambling now, so I better go.

Love to you all,
Roberta

I knew that I was going to stay in Washington with Brian no matter what he said. I told him that, and the relief on his face strengthened my resolve to be there for him for as long as he needed me. I talked with Paul about this and let him know that I would stay indefinitely. He needed to get back to Boston and his job, but promised he would be back in a few weeks. We actually worked out a plan to do ten days on and ten days off. We were not sure how it would work but thought it would be worth a try. We spoke to "Moscow" in Family Assistance about it and she agreed to help us give it a try. I don't know her last name but she made things happen and was always there with a smile and a hug. The paper work was mind numbing, but we did it.

While there in DC, we were officially Brian's Non-Medical Attendants. We never would have been able to do this without the Army paying for the flights back and forth. That would have been too expensive for either of us. We were very grateful for that help.

The "Family Assistance" meeting that we were required to attend was every Monday (I think – it's hard to remember, things just blur together some days). I think they did a fairly good job of explaining what was out there for help for Brian and for us. But at that point, I was still overwhelmed with the whole situation, and not much sank in. I brought a notebook with me to take notes, but I didn't. I couldn't. I was not capable of actually thinking. I was running on pure emotion and adrenalin. I keep thinking that the Army had to know that we were like zombies. The "newbies". That's what we were. You could tell who had been here for a while and who had just arrived. We all had that same look on our faces. It's hard to describe, but it was a look that I became very familiar with.

From the beginning, Brian experienced phantom pain. It was difficult to understand and comprehend, and it was difficult to watch him suffer through it. The first time he was able to describe it to me, he told me that it was like cramming his feet into boots that were two sizes too small, and his toes were jammed up inside the boots. He did not know what to do for it, and the hospital staff encouraged him to take meds. He hated that because they made him feel so groggy and out of it, and he did not like that feeling.

Eventually, he would learn some tricks to help deal with the phantom pain. One was to stimulate other parts of his leg, including his stumps, by repeatedly striking the ends of his legs, gently but firmly, with a rolled up towel. It sort of confused his brain into forgetting the phantom pain as it focused on the sensations from Brian hitting his legs. He used that technique a lot. I also would massage his stumps, that would help sometimes. I really enjoyed doing that for him. It made me feel useful, and I could see that he liked having that done. Many amputees told Brian that the phantom pain would never completely go away. Some told him that they experienced it just a few times a year now, but that it was difficult to deal with.

Fri, 23 Jun 2006 17:52

Hi everyone,

I have to apologize. I have been sending out updates, but apparently no one is getting them. I figured out what I was doing wrong, (duh) so here goes…

Brian is doing well. Actually he is the talk of the hospital and physical therapy department. He is incredibly motivated, and determined to get back up and walk again. His surgery on Tuesday went very well. The blood clot that he has was not an issue or problem as they put a filter in one of his main arteries to block it from going to the heart. They are giving him Coumadin and he will be on it for six months. Today, he had to have a transfusion with two pints of blood. He lost a lot during the initial explosion and in surgery as well and his red blood cell count was extremely low.

He was aggravated because they would not let him do PT (physical therapy) or OT (occupational therapy). He looked better afterwards so hopefully all is well there. They also put what they call "shrink wraps" on his legs. They are like surgical stockings, but look like ace bandages. The purpose of them is to help reduce the swelling and give him some support. He is way ahead of the program for putting them on. I was actually taught to put them on for him and I saw his stumps for the first time today. I must say, it was not as bad as I had expected.

He had a visit from General Casey, the big cheese in Iraq, who was here for a while visiting the troops in Walter Reed. Leave it to Brian, but he was telling the General what is wrong in Iraq. It's amazing the amount of visitors he gets in one day. We have been told to expect a lot more the closer it gets to July 4th.

Anyway, I hope this email reaches everyone. I'm exhausted, but doing well. Paul and Cassie have gone home and it's just Brian and me, but we are managing. I stayed with him last night, but I'm at the hotel tonight for a good night's sleep. Hopefully!!!

Keep the prayers coming.

Love,
Roberta

Everywhere we went, whether physical or occupational therapy, or just wandering around the hospital, Brian was already well known. They were all talking about how well he was doing, and the speed in which he was recovering. He seemed to have such a positive attitude; I wondered where it came from. After all he had been through, I can't imagine him being as positive as he was. Things would change, but for now, he was doing great.

The whole blood clot issue became worrisome for me as my family has a gene that makes a person prone to blood clots. I wanted him to be tested for it. I spoke to Amanda, his physical medicine and rehabilitation doctor, and gave her the information to be tested. Some of my sisters are on Coumadin and will be for life. Being on that drug is life altering, but he really had no choice. Blood clots were common with his type of injury, and hopefully, that was all it was.

The day before they gave him the transfusion, I knew he needed something. He looked drawn and pale; his face was beginning to look sunken in. I spoke to his nurse about the way he looked. After the transfusion, he looked so much better. Then we had to deal with the shrink wraps. They were like girdles or binders for his stumps to help with the swelling and to shape them for the prosthetics. It's difficult to describe how they had to be put on. You couldn't just put them on like a pair of stockings, because Brian would have gone crazy with pain. So how they did it was to invert them one at a time onto an open ended tube a little larger than an oatmeal container, and then gently slide it onto his stump. It was pretty ingenious actually, and not very easy to do. It was difficult to put it on the tube. But once they were on, he said his legs felt much better. The support that they gave his legs was comforting to him.

At this point, Paul and Cassie and the baby went home. I encouraged them to go. The days were getting routine and he was no longer critical. We were settling into a routine. It was quicker than expected, but a routine none the less. I have to say that I was glad that they left. I missed them when they were gone, especially Haley, but I was glad to see them go. I worried about everyone while they were there. It's my nature to do that. But I really did not have the strength to keep it up. Brian took all my strength. My worries and thoughts and fears, they were all with him. There was only so much of me to go around.

Haley was amazing while she was there with us. She brought smiles to so many faces throughout the day. She was not that comfortable with "Granpa" yet and cried when he took her so Cass and I could visit with Brian. People would come up to me when I had her and ask if she was the little one that was crying with the older man?! I got such a kick out of that. She now loves to visit Granpa. She made Brian smile and that was worth a million bucks to me. My nickname for him has always been, "my smiling friend". When I would write to him wherever he was, I would address the letter, "Hey, my smiling friend", and end it with, "take care of yourself, my smiling friend". Funny, but I cannot remember how or why I started calling him that.

Sun, 25 Jun 2006 15:49

Hi all,

It was kind of a gloomy day here in DC. It rained most of the morning and was cloudy and muggy. Brian and I went to the BBQ at the Mologne House. There were motorcycles on display, Customs Enforcement puppies in training, and food. We didn't stay long though. Brian tires easily and I don't think he was ready for the public in general. He is anxious to get back into PT. They do a shortened program on Saturday and nothing on Sunday. The weekends drag here. He watched a movie in the afternoon and I read.

They have him on Klonopin for the phantom pain and it does help with that, but it makes him drowsy, dizzy, and blurs his vision. He hates it so he is going to talk to his doctor in the morning about taking something else. He is on a lot of meds but hopefully they can figure out what works the best for him.

That's about it here. I will update in a few days. Keep the prayers coming.

Love,
Roberta

To say the weekends drag was an understatement. It was positively dead at the hospital, and at the Mologne House. There were very few people around and it was very quiet. The hospital was like a ghost town. The Dunkin Donuts in the hospital shut down on the weekends. How bad is that??!! I came to hate the weekends for a while because there was nothing for Brian or me to do. He was so busy during the week, it was hard to adjust to the weekends. I know the rest was good for both of us, but when there was nothing to do, we both had too much time to think. And thinking could get us in trouble.

Brian was battling depression, and anger, and PTSD. He suffered a Traumatic Brain Injury (TBI) and I did not feel he was getting any treatment for it. He wasn't exactly seeking treatment either. That was not the "Army way". Over time though, he came to realize that the Army way was not always the right way. He eventually hooked up with a good psychiatrist and is being treated for TBI. Hopefully, he will get beyond that and recover.

I always think too much. And when I have nothing to do, it's even worse. I worried about everything, and the weekends seem to bring out the best in me. Most of it was focused on Brian, but I worried about how things were going at home and at work. It was very difficult to be separated from my husband, Chet. I did not like not knowing what was happening at home. I was sure that the house was falling apart and in a state of total chaos. I was wrong about that though. They seemed to manage pretty well without me.

At night time, I tried to distract myself by reading. It was not easy though because I could not concentrate on much. I wandered around the hotel just looking for someone to talk to and I almost always found somebody. I was surprised to find young mothers doing laundry late at night. Come to find out, their babies were sick with different types of cancers. I encouraged them to talk because they all seemed so lonely. Most of the time they were separated from their husband and other children. They were there for the treatments while the rest of their families were at their husband's duty station, wherever that was. While I could barely remember their names, I learned a lot about them and their children. They were so strong (and they had to be), because their children were so young and so sick. With cancer, you just don't know if they will survive or not. I knew Brian would survive. I knew he would never go back to Iraq. I hoped and prayed that he would rise above his injuries and make a new and happy life for himself.

Tue, 27 Jun 2006 17:41

Hi everyone,

Just wanted to let you know things are going well. Brian had a good day today with PT, and the OT was canceled. I think he was glad because he was able to get some stuff done, mostly paperwork and personal business, but he was glad to get to it. One of the doctors on the prosthetic team was talking with me today, and I said that I thought Brian was doing really well. He said, "Are you kidding me, he is doing great! He is the talk of the hospital staff with the progress he is making." He went on to tell me that Brian was an extraordinary young man... That's not a term I might use on him, but hey, what can I say.

I also wanted to address another issue with everyone. I have been asked by so many people what they can do for Brian, what he needs, or what does he want. To be honest, he is pretty much set right now. Between Paul, myself, Cassie and Anthony we pretty much got everything he needed. Which leads me to this.

If you really want to do something, you could send donations to the Red Cross here at the hospital, or to the Mologne House. The Red Cross does great work here and they go out of their way to get items for the patients here that they may need. Those items include t-shirts, boxers, briefs, boxer briefs, gym shorts, nylon shorts, socks, baseball hats. Any sizes, any colors. The Soldiers really have no clothing when they come here except the hospital gowns. Most of them, within a short period of time, start to venture out of their rooms for PT, OT or just to the cafeteria. So clothing like that is good. Snacks are good as well.

And at the Mologne House, where I am staying, it's a hotel, and most of the Soldiers come here when they get to outpatient status, as will Brian. And people bring things here all the time – like clothing, books, movies, magazines, etc. And they always get taken by Soldiers that need them. So if you wanted to do that, or let the Red Cross know that you are donating in Brian's name – that would be great. The address is: *Make a financial donation to Armed Forces Emergency Services by calling 1-800-RED CROSS. Contributions may be sent to the American Red Cross Armed Forces Emergency Services, P.O. Box 91820, Washington, DC 20090. Internet users can make a secure online contribution by visiting www.redcross.org.*

And that's my story and I'm sticking to it. Oh yes, Brian almost met Dave Matthews yesterday, but we did see him in the hallway. Today Brian refused to see a Marine general. He kills me. He has nothing against Marines or generals; he was just in one of his moods. Keep the prayers coming. I'm tentatively scheduled to come home on July 5. I will be home for ten days, and Paul will be here for Brian. I should find out for sure tomorrow.

Love,
Roberta

The paperwork. The huge amount of paperwork. Everywhere we went, everything we did, involved tons of paperwork. I'm quite certain that Brian still has tons more to fill out before this is over with. Some of the paperwork I could help him with, but some he was pretty much on his own. I cannot understand why it has to be so difficult. But the military makes it that way, and that's the way it will stay. Whenever Brian had to have surgery, whether it was a cut down or just a wash out, or anything simple, the paperwork was overwhelming. When he became an outpatient, it was horrible. He would spend one whole day doing things necessary for the surgery the following day. Drawing blood, paperwork, getting weighed, paperwork, blood pressure, paperwork, it was never ending. And Brian had to go through this so many times. He is still going through it. It was always hurry up and wait. It will always be that. That is the Army way.

When he became an outpatient and needed prescriptions refilled, if he came with me to the pharmacy, they would flag him and move him to the front of the line. The amount of people filling prescriptions at the pharmacy was astounding. But if I just went for him when he was not feeling well, or just because it was too difficult to make the trip to the pharmacy from the Mologne House, I would have to wait usually an hour at least before it got refilled.

And God forbid if we forgot to refill something in time. Then we were screwed. Brian would get angry and I would feel guilty for not remembering. I felt bad for him because I had a hard time remembering things. I still do. One day he asked me to put his sunglasses in my purse when we got to the hospital. When we left later that day to head back to the Mologne House, he asked me for them. I told him that I did not have them. He told me that he gave them to me when we got to the hospital that morning. I argued with him for a few minutes and to prove him wrong, went into my purse to show him that they were not there. Of course, there they were sitting in my purse. I had no memory of him giving them to me. How bizarre is that – to forget that and be so sure that I did not have them. My head was full of so much that I just did not remember that. He was frustrated with me and I cannot blame him. I was frustrated with myself.

Wed, 28 Jun 2006 16:58

Hi Everyone,

Just a quick update. During occupational therapy today, Brian's therapist took him on a little field trip. Brian wheeled his way from the hospital all the way to the hotel. And let me tell you, a lot of that was uphill. I don't know how he did it, but he did. Then they came to my hotel room to figure out how Brian can get his wheelchair into the bathroom. They were able to figure it out, but I have put in for a handicap accessible room. Hopefully that will come soon. They are talking about releasing him from the hospital, maybe on the weekend!! That is totally amazing and pretty much unheard of here to get out that quick. I just hope he isn't rushing too much, but that's the Mom in me. He is looking forward to sleeping in a real bed. (Wait until he hears me snoring, LOL)

He gets his rental wheelchair tomorrow, which is a bit better than the hospital one, and he will get fitted for a brand new one designed for him. He won't start the prosthesis process until the stitches come out and the swelling has gone away, but he is pretty close to it.

I truly believe everyone's prayers are what is helping him and what is giving him the strength to do this, so please, please, keep them coming.

Needless to say, after the strenuous day he had, he is in some pain and very tired. He told me last night he slept throughout the night for the first time; I hope he does tonight. I hope I do also. That's all for now.

Love,
Roberta

Brian's occupational therapist, Oren, is a funny guy. He has a good sense of humor and knows when to use it. He is good with his patients and Brian liked him from the beginning. I had my doubts though when he made Brian wheel all the way from the 3rd floor of the hospital to the Mologne House. It is a very hilly journey, especially in a wheelchair. He would not let me help him and it was a difficult trip for Brian and for me. Brian was soaked in sweat when we got to the hotel and I was totally frazzled. I kept joking with Oren that he was so mean to Brian. Deep down, I thought he was but I knew that he had to do that. I knew that Brian needed to be able to travel back and forth between the hotel and the hospital. I knew all those things, but it was so hard to watch him struggle.

Oren was there in case his chair started to tip over, which was entirely possible given the terrain there. Once we got to the hotel, we had to find out if Brian could maneuver his wheelchair in the hotel room. The room itself was very spacious and seemed roomier than other rooms (it was a corner room), but the bathroom was not handicapped accessible. Brian could get into the bathroom, and with great difficulty he could shut the door, but it was not really an ideal situation for him. I called down to the front desk and requested a handicapped accessible room. It would take a few days, but I knew we would get one. It seemed weird that all the rooms there were not accessible, but it was the same way at the hospital. Brian could not use the bathroom in his room. He had to go down the hallway to use another bathroom that was accessible. It didn't make sense, and it still doesn't make sense…

MY SON IS ALIVE...

ALMOST AN OUTPATIENT

Thu, 29 Jun 2006 16:10

Hi all,

Well, an amazing thing has happened today. The doctors talked things over with Brian and they all decided he could become an outpatient tomorrow. I have to tell you, I am a little nervous. I asked him afterwards, when we were back in his room, if he really thought he was ready. He said he didn't know if he was, but he was willing to give it a go. He is tired of the lack of privacy at the hospital and the constant stream of visitors. Today it was the Prime Minister of Japan. That entailed the Secret Service, bomb sniffing dogs, the Japanese version of the Secret Service, and MP's everywhere – it was a pain in the butt. Who knows who will be there tomorrow? Could be the President of Timbucktoo...

Anyway, we talked it over and agreed to take things one hour at a time. Little baby steps, so to speak, until we figure things out and figure out what works for him. He will go to PT and OT five or six days a week and I think he has to actually report to formation at 7:30 Monday through Friday mornings. I guess he will find all of that out tomorrow.

He also may have to give himself a shot until his blood levels with the Coumidin are right. Thank goodness that will be just for six months, because of the blood clot. And then when the stitches come out in a week or so, he will start the fitting process for his first set of legs. So that will consume a lot of time as well. He is going to be busy.

We have a new address... They will send any mail that goes to the hospital over to here. Cards are appreciated.

He has actually helped a couple of young men here. The wife of one thanked me today for raising such a wonderful young man. He knows this guy from his battalion and he knew about the explosion that wounded him the week before Brian got wounded. He had been unconscious for a while, and didn't know what happened. Brian told him everything, and his wife told me that it helped him to know what had happened, because no one really knew.

The other guy was having a bad day today and his dad asked Brian to come in and meet him. They got to talking and his Dad told me that was what he needed – another Soldier to talk to. They all seem to help each other out. It is definitely a special "club" that they all belong to here. The walking/wheeling wounded.

There was a couple outside the Mologne House when I got back earlier, and I had the feeling they had been here for a while. The husband's leg was badly injured and he has one of those halo's on it. Anyway, I asked them if I could talk to them and get some advice on where we should try to get a room here. The room I am in isn't handicapped accessible so we need to move somewhere else. We are on a waiting list. Anyway, they told me to stick to the 1st and 2nd floors because wheelchairs can exit those floors without assistance or without using the elevator. They said that if there were a fire and he was on the 3rd or 4th floor, how would we get him out if you can't use the elevator in case of fire?? I would never have thought of that.

What I am trying to say is that they were pleased to give me advice, just as several other people have. As a newbie, I was grateful for any advice at all. They show me shortcuts to the hospital, where to get the best buys on things, or how to get them for nothing, and all kinds of information that you need to be here.

Every day I check in with the front desk to see if there is a room available. Until then, Brian and I will make do. The front desk does not know how I will haunt them until we get a handicap room, but they are going to find out.

Wow, I didn't mean to go on this much. I have a lot of nervous energy. Can you tell? I miss everyone back home. I did get my flight on the 5th of July, and I think I arrive at 11 or so, at Boston's Logan Airport. I will be home until the 14th. I plan on going to work some while I'm home, but mostly just trying to be normal – for what that's worth anyway!!

Take care everyone and keep the prayers coming.

Love,
Roberta

I have to tell you, I was scared silly about Brian being discharged. I was afraid that medically he was not ready and I would not be able to handle being his non medical attendant. That is the term the Army used to describe family members who stay with the injured Soldiers after they become outpatients. His dressings needed to be changed and medication doled out. He was on so many different pills I was sure I would not be able to handle it. I had a hard enough time remembering to take my own meds, never mind all of his. I almost wanted to try and talk him out of it, but in the end it was not necessary. I kept telling myself that the hospital was close by if we needed anything. I had seen a few people being taken by ambulance back to the hospital for one reason or another.

I was surprised that he was willing to speak to other Soldiers. He was suffering a lot with pain, real and phantom, and with his own demons. He put on a brave front in front of other people, but when we were alone in his room, or anywhere, his guard would come down and I could see he was suffering. I knew that he had to work this out mostly by himself, but I let him know that I was always going to be there for him if, or when, he needed me. He was concerned about some of the Soldiers there and he would check on them frequently.

He was very good to some of the parents as well – encouraging them and trying to give them some hope. He would tell them that he had been hurt only two and a half weeks ago and look how good he was doing. He didn't let them see the pain that he was in.

I met some wonderful people there, people who were going through exactly what I was. We were starved for someone to talk to – someone who would listen to our story, and have one to tell in return. We compared notes on everything, from our son's injuries, to the best place to grocery shop, the quickest way to get over to the hospital each morning, and the best place to eat lunch. One Mom, Faye, must have seen something in me, because one day she convinced me to sign up for a guided tour of DC. It was free, they provided lunch, and it was a chance to get away from the hospital for just a little while. It was a bus tour of DC and we also went to Arlington Cemetery. For the first time, I saw the changing of the guards at the Tomb of the Unknown Soldiers. It was very inspiring and very emotional for me.

Faye and I became friends and shared rides to the PX to grocery shop. She quickly found out tons of information about anything and everything there. She was a vast wealth of information and shared it with everyone. She helped so many people, I thought she should have become the mayor of our little world there. I don't know where she got her strength, but I was able to draw on some of it from just being around her.

Fri, 30 Jun 2006 12:05

Hi all,

Well, I guess we jumped the gun a bit too soon. Brian won't be leaving the hospital today. He had a bad night and morning with pain. His nerve endings were on overload and it took a while before we could figure out what worked to calm them down. He was in a lot of pain and I felt helpless. It wasn't a good morning but he is doing better now. He is taking his first shower in forever, so that will cheer him up.

They gave him a four day pass to go wherever he wants or to stay here at the hotel for the night. He has the option to go back to the hospital if the pain gets to be too much. I think we are both a little relieved, to be honest. And I still haven't gotten the handicap room yet here at the Mologne House. I'm going down in a minute to check on one. They also gave us taxi vouchers, so if he is up to it, we will go to a mall or a restaurant over the weekend. We are going to just take it as it comes and play it by ear.

I fell apart earlier when he was in all that pain. I felt bad because it makes him feel bad. It's just frustrating to see him suffer like that and not be able to help. From what we have learned, the phantom pain decreases a great deal when he gets his fittings and has a cap to wear on his legs. That will happen in a week or so when the stitches come out.

Gotta go and check on rooms. Keep the prayers coming.

Love,
Roberta

Boy, did I fall apart. I just could not stop crying. He was in agony and it was written all over his face. He began to realize that most of the pain was phantom, but just recognizing that fact did not make it any better. He got some good advice from the therapists, but he was just learning how to deal with it and it was very overwhelming. My heart was breaking and I could not stop the tears once they started. I left his room and walked the halls. People were kind and talked with me but I was at a loss to stop the grief.

At that point, it was grief – raw and uncontrolled grief. The anger came later. And it's still with me. I can't seem to get past that. I'm working on it, but it's going to take some time. I can't imagine how hard it must be for Brian. Eventually, I made my way outside and called my best friend Ellen. I knew she would make me feel better and she did. It was so hot out there though. You could not use most cell phones inside the hospital. There was just no reception there at all. That was a big problem for Brian and for me. He could call us from Iraq, but he couldn't make calls from the hospital in Washington, DC. How strange is that?

Sun, 2 Jul 2006 15:14

Hi Everyone,

It's been pretty much a quiet day today. Yesterday Brian wanted to venture out so we took a taxi to a mall in Montgomery County and spent about three or four hours there. He got some clothes, books, a watch, and cologne, among other things. He also wanted to eat out somewhere and, of all places, he chose McDonalds. Go figure.

He did ok with the trip – a little bothered by people's stares. It doesn't bother him when children stare but it does when adults do. By the time we got back to the hospital, he was exhausted and starting to have some good pain, so we got him medicated right away. He told me this morning that he slept pretty good most of the night.

Today we stayed in his room all day. He was tired and seemed to just want to hang there. He played his computer games most of the day and I read and slept. Then we had a visitor. We got our picture taken with James Gandolfini, from the Sopranos. He talked to Brian about a place in Maine that he is inviting some of the Soldiers to. It seems he wants them to write about their experiences, if they want to, and then something may be developed from whatever they write. I don't know if he is talking about a TV show or a movie, but he is interested in hearing their stories. Brian was invited to come, and James gave him his cell phone number for Brian to call him whenever. You just never know who is going to "pop in" there.

I came back to the hotel early. My back is killing me. I miss my Jacuzzi. Chet better have that in tip top shape when I get home! I am coming home Wednesday morning, and will be home until the 14th. I may try to push my return flight back a couple of days if possible. Paul comes in tomorrow and will be here until the 16th. Brian is excited because Paul is getting a rental car and they plan on seeing some of the sights while he is here.

I got a couple of emails about his address and right now it's still at the hospital. By Wednesday, it will probably be the Mologne House. I will keep you all posted.

That's about it here. I hear thunder again outside. They have some doozy thunder storms here.

Keep the prayers coming.

Love,
Roberta

The trip to the mall was traumatic for me. He seemed ok most of the time, but I was a wreck. When you are dealing with wheelchairs, your whole method of movement is off. I did not want him to become tired too soon so I pushed him in his chair. As we shopped and accumulated things, it got more difficult to balance everything. It was just that it was new to us – awkward and frustrating. I wanted it to feel like a normal day at the mall, but that was not how it was.

It was funny though. The more I tried, the harder it seemed. But then he wanted to stop into a Spencer's and just check things out. It turned out that the clerk that waited on him had gone to school with an old girlfriend of Brian's. It was funny, but that connection made him feel like his old self. That was something I was not able to do. It brought us back to reality, so to speak. I think we both felt that we were so far from reality that we would never feel normal again. That clerk brought us back to earth!!

It took a while for the taxi to come to the mall to pick us up. We were both a little worried and frustrated. He was able to transfer himself without too much difficulty and I was happy that he could. It would have been very hard if someone had to lift him to and from the wheelchair. I was so relieved when we got back to the hospital. I knew he had reached the end of his endurance for that trip. We pushed it an hour or so longer than we should have. In time I would get to know the signals that told me he was ready to stop doing whatever it was we were doing and call it a day.

While walking through the mall, an older gentleman came up to Brian and put his hand out to shake Brian's hand. He shook his hand

and just said, "Thank You". I know that Brian was humbled by that experience. The gentleman was dignified and solemn, almost formal as he shook Brian's hand. There was also another elderly man who saluted Brian as we passed by him. To me, I felt that they were probably war veterans who recognized a fellow Soldier when they saw one. It was amazing that Brian got to experience a "grateful nation" as opposed to what happened to the Soldiers returning from Vietnam.

The next day, we just stayed in Brian's hospital room. Both of us were worn out from the day before and just could not bring ourselves to do or to go anywhere. The visit from James Gandolfini was funny. Now that I think back on it, I had never really watched the Sopranos but heard a lot about them from various sources, including the Imus in The Morning Show on talk radio. So I was a bit impressed with having a visit from him. It was funny, but all of the celebrities that we met while at Walter Reed were so down to earth and charming. Through it all, I kept thinking that I should have one of those autograph books that you have when you are visiting Disneyland!

Tues, 4 Jul 2006 06:56

Hi everyone,

Happy 4th of July to all! Cassie, Anthony, and My Little Pumpkin, Haley, came yesterday! And Brian's dad, Paul, arrived as well. It was a whirlwind kind of day as they wanted to take Brian out and show him some fun. It was a long day to say the least. We ended it by having dinner at the Legal Seafood right in DC. It was actually in Georgetown. The wait was a long time so Paul made a phone call to someone in Boston, who in turn called the guy who owns Legal Seafood, who in turn called the restaurant in DC, and they seated us right away. They also gave us complimentary appetizers. Then a Navy Commander wanted to buy us a round of drinks in Brian's honor.

Brian had the biggest lobster I have ever seen. It was funny watching him eat it. It was very late by the time we got him back to the hospital. He said he didn't want to do anything today, except just rest. I have to watch out that they don't wear him out in their enthusiasm to do things with him and for him.

I'm flying home tomorrow morning. I can't wait. It will be hard to leave Brian, but I do know that I need to come home for a while. I need a break. I'm planning on working while I am home. I think it will help me get into the routine of things by doing that. So maybe I will see some of you while I am home. If not, I'm sure we will "chat".

Please keep your prayers coming and I will keep the updates coming from home.

Love,
Roberta

I was so happy to have Cassie and Haley back with me. I missed them both a lot. Haley is very good company for me. She is such a sweet baby. We all stayed in the same hotel room. It was a bit crowded, but we managed. Paul slept at the hospital with Brian so that made it a bit easier. The day before they came, I was able to get a handicapped room on the 2nd floor. I was happy that he would be able to have a comfortable place when he became an outpatient.

We ended up going to a mall near the Pentagon. It was strange to see the building with my own eyes. There were signs of construction there, but it was definitely the "Pentagon". Brian wanted to get some dress clothes for Haley's christening. Cassie and I let the boys shop on their own. When they were finished, Brian showed us the nice outfit he got for the christening. It was then when Cassie asked him if he remembered to buy dress socks to match his outfit. She did not realize what she had said until Brian (in true brotherly fashion) punched her in the arm. She apologized a million times. I know that she felt bad, but to me, it was as if she did not see him as having no feet. She still saw him in the same way that she always saw him. I thought that was a good thing. I think Brian did as well, but he, of course, wanted to make his sister feel bad! Some things never change!

I was a wreck, as usual, by the time we had gotten to the Legal Seafood. I could tell Brian was pretty much at his end and ready to go back. If Paul had not made that phone call, I was going to go up to the hostess, explain the situation, and do whatever it took to get us seated. There were tons of restaurants within walking distance, and we checked them out, but they were all just as crowded as Legal Seafood. I felt bad for Brian. He really wanted to eat and enjoy food that he hadn't had in forever, but he was getting sicker by the minute. Anthony took him outside for fresh air after a while and it seemed to help him a lot. He definitely could not eat as much as he used to.

Tue, 4 Jul 2006 16:10

Hi all,

What a busy day at the hospital today. We had a visit from Jason Alexander (George from Seinfeld), from Nicolette Sheridan and Michael Bolton, and a couple of Army Generals. They were all very nice and spent quite a bit of time talking with Brian and with us. It was interesting. We had the opportunity to go to the fireworks display at the National Mall, but chose not to. Brian did not think that he would be able to handle the noise from the fireworks. I thought that just being out there with the heat, the noise, and the crowd would be too much for him and for me.

My flight is in the morning. I'm anxious to be home, yet anxious about leaving Brian.

Keep us in your thoughts and prayers.

Love,
Roberta

Brian's room got changed at the hospital. It was a four bed room, but only one other guy was in it. It had a handicapped bathroom; Brian wanted that. He hated having to go down the hall to take a shower or use the bathroom. He was so happy that he did not have to use the commode or a urinal anymore, and with the handicapped bathroom, it was easier for him to transfer. It took a while to move everything. He had already accumulated so much. Just as we got settled, the visitors started arriving. I really was impressed with most of them. They were kind and gracious and genuinely interested in what Brian had to say.

July 4th was the day that I began to think that Brian would be ok, that he would still be the same guy he was when he left for Iraq. He was fooling around with his sister, playing with Haley, and just being a clown. He hooked one arm over the bar that goes across the top of the hospital bed and lifted himself up. He was swinging back and forth, making monkey gestures and noises. We all laughed long and hard, including him. Paul took pictures of him doing that. One of them eventually ended up in the newspapers.

I had an early flight, so I said goodbye to Brian that night. It was difficult. I kept telling him I would be back, and if he needed me, I would be back in an instant. He kept thanking me for being there for him. I told him that I would not have been anywhere else – I could not have been anywhere else.

I cried when the plane took off from Reagan Airport. As strange as it sounds, it was beginning to feel like home to me. By the time it landed in Boston at Logan Airport, I was doing better. I had Chet pick me up at the Braintree bus terminal, so it would be easier on him. I was so happy to see him, it felt like we had been apart forever – almost three weeks. But I still felt like I should be with Brian. I felt like no one could take care of him as good as I would, and I know that was crazy. I know his Dad would take just as good care of him, but I felt helpless not being there. I wanted to know what he was doing and what was going on. I wanted to know what was happening with Faye and Nick, Sandy and Jeff and Jeremiah. I worried that the room at the Mologne House was a mess, because they were being slobs. I worried about everything. I physically ached to be back in DC with Brian. But I did know that I needed a break. I was so conflicted.

Wed, 5 Jul 2006 15:24

Hi everyone,

I'm back. It was tough leaving him, but I am glad I did. I need to recharge my batteries. I plan on going back to work while I am home and get into my normal routine for a while. I missed Chet and being in my own home.

I talked to Brian this afternoon. He is doing a trial sleepover at the Mologne House tonight and depending on how that goes, he may be discharged tomorrow. He said that they worked him hard in PT and OT. They know what is best for him.

I am going back the 16th of this month but I am home now and will enjoy it while I can.

Thank you all so much for your thoughts and prayers. They have given me strength and courage to face the future with Brian. He is going to be fine, I know. It may be a bit of a bumpy ride to get there, but he will get there. Mark my words…

Love,
Roberta

PS - I will continue with the updates if you want me to.

I already had my return flight booked. What does that tell you? I must say that the Army was very good about our flights back and forth. It was unusual for both parents to split their time being non medical attendants, but that is what we did. It worked out very good for the both of us. The Army not only paid for the flights back and forth, but they paid us while we were there with Brian. It certainly helped having them do that. I was able to keep up with my monthly bills back home and have money for food and whatever while I was in DC. The paperwork to accomplish this was a challenge. But that is a story for another day.

Meanwhile, I am home and I am determined to enjoy being here. I saw as many friends and family as I could and I went to work. It was a day filled with hugs and talk of Brian. Everyone wanted to know how he was doing and how I was doing.

Things had changed while I was gone. My job became something that I was not used to and it took me a while to grasp it. I felt guilty though. I knew I was going back in a week or so, and I felt like I was leaving them at a time when they really needed me. But I had no choice, my son needed me.

Thu, 6 Jul 2006 17:02

Hi all,

I just got off the phone with Brian. He wasn't too chatty – he was downright grumpy. He can't get his laptop to work in the hotel room. He has come to depend on that and he isn't happy about not being able to use it. They will figure it out though.

He is not officially an outpatient yet, but he has been sleeping at the hotel the last couple of nights. He loves the body pillow, Sue. Thank you so much for sending it.

Speaking of sending, he asked me to let everyone know that he appreciates everything, but no more candy please, he is swimming in it. He had his eyes examined today and was told he needs glasses for distance. The stitches will come out by Monday at the latest and the fittings will begin. He had PT and OT today and they worked him good. He was "smoked" as he puts it. I worry that he isn't eating right, but I talked with Paul and he assured me he is. Paul said Brian misses me. I miss him.

I went to work today and did enjoy being back. They enjoyed having me back as well. It felt good to get into the swing of things there. They hired two people to do my work while I was gone.

That's about it here. I'm happy to be home, but at the same time I wish I was with Brian. I'm going to relax and enjoy some quiet time here at home.

Keep the prayers coming.

Love,
Roberta

I can't tell you how much I worried about him when I wasn't there. It was awful. I knew that Paul would take good care of him, but they are guys, and sometimes they don't always do what is best for them. I wanted to call a hundred times a day, but knew that I couldn't. I had so many worries going through my head. I was very nervous about his mental state. He put on a brave front for people, but I could see how much he was suffering. I could hear it in his voice – it broke my heart. He felt guilty about the explosion. He felt guilty that another Soldier got hurt. He was most concerned with his "men" who were still over in Iraq fighting the battle.

He was also dealing with a broken relationship with someone he cared a great deal for. She was not who he thought she was, and he had just broken off the relationship before the IED. She came to see him while he was in the hospital. I was prepared to keep her from hurting him, no matter what it took. He wanted to see her face to face though, so he could end things in person. I was amazed that he had the strength to do that given what he was going through.

There was also the very attractive young nurse in ICU who paid extra attention to Brian, the one who gave him her St. Christopher medal to wear. She seemed to be genuinely concerned for him and would visit him in his room on Ward 57 at least once a day. He enjoyed her company and they talked about doing things outside the hospital. One night they had planned to go out to dinner, but she called later in the afternoon and canceled saying she had forgotten she was supposed to be with a friend that night. Brian and I ended up going out to dinner, and of all the places in the world to go, we ran into her. She was with another guy, not a girlfriend. Brian was angry but turned his anger inward, as he tended to do. He returned her necklace the next day and that was that.

Sat, 8 Jul 2006 11:04

Hey everyone,

I must say, it's good to be home. Just to get into the routine of normal life feels good. I can't wait to get back to DC though. Brian called me yesterday afternoon. He got the stitches out and said it was very painful, but it is done. He will start the process of being fitted for his caps. By the end of the week, he should have a pair of legs and be walking at the parallel bars at PT. He is pretty excited about that. He sounded tired and his voice was strained, but he assures me he is doing fine and is eating well…blah blah blah… The mother in me.

That's about it for now. I'm home until next Sunday and I don't know how long I will be there this time.

Thank you all for the prayers and good thoughts.

Love,
Roberta

It was good to be home, even though I wondered constantly what he was doing. I would look at the clock and say, "It's 10:00am, he must be at PT right now". All day long I followed his routine from a distance. I wanted to call a million times, but I didn't. I remembered how aggravated I got sometimes when my cell rang when we were in PT or OT. It's silly, but it felt like an intrusion. We were so focused on his therapy, we did not want to be bothered. It was like that when visitors came to PT, which they did all the time. Except for Tom and his wife. He was the Korean War vet who came every Thursday to visit with the Soldiers in Ward 57 and 58 and in PT and OT as well. Tom lost both legs from below his knees in the Korean War, and his wife was his nurse while in the hospital there. They fell in love and have been together ever since. Tom is like a grandfather to all of the Soldiers there, and his wife bakes delicious goodies for everyone. Tom's spirit and strength show the injured and wounded Soldiers that it is possible to live a normal life, no matter what their injuries were. He is an inspiration to them all, and they all love him.

What I enjoyed about being home was being with my husband, Chet. I missed sleeping beside him at night. I missed just having him to talk to during dinner. Dinner in DC was always an adventure, but not always a good one. I missed cooking and doing laundry at home. I missed my house, my bed, my Jacuzzi, my car, my job, and Curves. I had just started going a month before all this happened. I missed my regular, boring, routine life. Yet I still ached to be in DC with Brian. There were so many conflicting emotions and feelings that I did not know how to deal with. I just kept pushing them into the background – saving them for a rainy day, I guess.

Brian with Jason Alexander, "George" from Seinfeld – and Haley

GEN Richard Cody, Michael Bolton, Brian, and Nicolette Sheridan
July 4, 2006

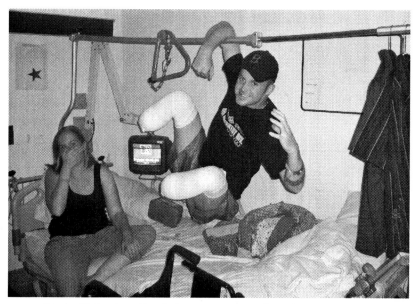

Brian "Monkey Boy" clowning around with sister Cassie

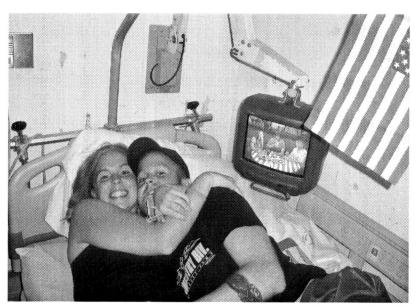

Brian and Cassie, still having fun

MY SON IS ALIVE...

WHEELCHAIR WRECK

Mon, 10 Jul 2006 15:45

Hi everyone,

It seems like it's been forever since I saw Brian. I know it hasn't, but it sure seems that way. He had quite an eventful weekend it seems. He was sightseeing with his Dad, Cassie, Anthony, and Haley. They were leaving the Iwo Jima Memorial and Brian was pushing himself in his wheelchair. He very seldom will let anyone push him. Anyway, the wheel of the chair got stuck in a crack in the pavement and the whole chair went over with Brian in it. He smacked his head pretty hard and hit the end of his left leg – very painful. They took him to the emergency room at Walter Reed and he got checked out. His left leg opened up a bit where the stitches were, but the doctors on duty didn't think that it needed to be stitched. Brian was angry with himself but made it through the rest of the weekend.

Because of the "crash" they were only able to cast his right leg today. The left leg is still open a bit and it needs to heal up, so it could be a week or two before they do that. But that might be a good thing, because he can get the feeling of one prosthetic leg at a time this way. He was pretty upset, but I think he has accepted it. He can't do anything about it anyway, so he just has to keep on working hard.

Cassie and Anthony and Haley went back to New York today. Brian told me he was going to miss them, but that he was glad, because it was a bit crowded in the hotel room with all of them there. Cassie is going to stay in NY till Haley's christening, which is now rescheduled to August 6. Brian intends to go to the christening as he is Haley's Godfather. I think the game plan is for him to fly there for the weekend. I don't know what I am doing or where I will be at that time, but I will just play it by ear, a theme of mine lately.

I don't think Brian will want or need me to stay with him much longer. I think he wants his privacy and wants to move ahead on his own.

That's pretty much it for now. I will post again when I have more information. This is going to be the hard part for him now. They will work him very hard in PT and OT. Keep him in your thoughts and prayers. He is going to need them for a while longer.

Love,
Roberta

We certainly did not know it then, but that "accident" in the wheel chair was the beginning of a long ordeal that is still going on now. His left leg has not been right since it happened. His right leg healed quickly and adapted to the prosthetic with very little trouble. The left leg, however, has been a painful ordeal for Brian. Continuous infections and almost constant pain is what he deals with now. He described the accident in detail to me. I cringe whenever I think about it.

When the wheelchair hit the crack in the pavement, it pitched forward and literally threw him out of the chair. He must have instinctively flailed his arms and legs trying to catch himself. His left leg slammed into the pavement pretty hard and he almost passed out from the pain. He did not want to go to the hospital though. Paul took him to the emergency room at Walter Reed and they seemed to think his left leg was ok. I believe that something needed to be done with it, and nothing was. His head also hit the pavement pretty hard. That was something that he did not need on top of everything else. He was already diagnosed with TBI (traumatic brain injury) and that fall did not help. I think every wounded warrior in Walter Reed had TBI. I am not trying to minimize it, what I am saying is that they all had some type of trauma to their bodies, and to their brain as well. It takes time for them both to recover. Sometimes they don't.

Most of the injuries were from IED explosions. Some were snipers. Others were from vehicle accidents. Needless to say, a TBI diagnosis was pretty much standard there. You could see it in their eyes if you looked closely. They all had a haunted look about them. Like they had seen and experienced way too much. As time went on, I saw that look begin to fade. I don't think they will ever lose it completely, but for most of them, it did get better.

Wed, 12 Jul 2006 09:48

Hi everyone,

I'm not sure who I told about Brian walking yesterday, but he did, sort of. He got a right prosthesis and walked using the parallel bars in PT. He was pretty excited. He said it did hurt somewhat, but he was happy to be "walking".

Then today he got some not so good news. They are afraid that the muscle on his left stump pulled away from the bone because of the accident he had in the wheelchair. If that happened it would never heal right. So on Monday they are going to open his incision area and make sure it's ok. This will obviously set him back some and he isn't too happy about it.

I'm flying out there Sunday morning. Paul talked to his doctor today. They are telling him that someone needs to be with him for a longer period of time. Brian may think he is ready to be on his own, but the doctors don't think so. So Paul and I are going to try and do a ten day on, ten day off routine and see how that works. In order to stay on the Army orders that we have, you can't be away for more than ten days at a time. It's kind of weird how that works, but that's the government for you.

My work has told me again to not worry about my job and take whatever time I need. Chet and I have a vacation planned for the last week of August and we plan on doing that.

So that's it from here. Gotta get back to work. Keep him in your prayers, please.

Love,
Roberta

This was the beginning of a long list of problems he had with his left leg, and he continues to have. It has been frustrating for him. I have seen him curse that leg and plead with that leg. The pain that he experienced with both legs, but mostly the left one, would make me cry. I can't pretend to know what he was going through, but I could see the agony written all over his face. There were times when there was nothing I could do for him except to leave him alone to deal with his agony and his pain, because it was his, and his alone. Nobody could know what he felt and what he was going through. Nobody could make it go away.

That was the most frustrating thing as a parent to go through – not to be able to help your child. No drugs, no magic pills, no soothing words were going to stop his pain. I prowled the halls of the Mologne House - the lobby, the front and back of the building, the cafeteria, the smoking area (even though I do not smoke). I thought that if I stayed in the room with him, I would not be able to conceal my anguish and would only end up making Brian feel bad because I felt bad. It was hard to know what to do. I had no experience here and nothing to fall back on.

Thu, 13 Jul 2006 16:47

Hi all,

It's been a rocky couple of days for Brian. He has been having some problems that were not expected. He had some type of seizure last night. He was with his Dad and he started shaking and blacked out momentarily. The doctors don't seem to be too concerned about it but, of course, I am worried. I guess it could be a lot of things but they are checking him daily with neuro checks and keeping a close eye on him. He is also experiencing some mental confusion, which can also be related to all of the above. I think he is pushing himself too hard so I am certain we are going to do "battle" when I get back to Washington. It will be interesting to say the least.

I leave on Sunday and I am trying to figure out how to get to Logan without using the tunnel system. I think I am probably going to just use the Braintree Logan Express so Chet doesn't have to drive me all the way in.

If anything comes up I will post and let you know. Otherwise, I will write when I get to Washington. Keep him in your prayers.

Love,
Roberta

It was hard getting reports second hand. I hate to say it but I think his Dad exaggerated a bit with the shaking episode. Or Brian just wanted me to believe that when I questioned him about it. I had seen this happen with his legs numerous times and it still happens now. The nerves go on overload and his leg just shakes uncontrollably. It takes some type of stimulation to make it stop. The blacking out, Brian said, was just him closing his eyes and not responding to his father. Only your child could get away with that. He was also on some pretty powerful drugs. Those alone would make most people comatose. They did not help much with the pain, especially the phantom pain, but they did take the edge off.

Of course, I just assumed once I got there everything would be ok and I would "fix" whatever was wrong. Boy was I naïve thinking like that.

Mon, 17 Jul 2006 14:20

Hi all,

Long day today with pre-op red tape. It took over five hours to do things that really should only take 45 minutes. That's the Army way I guess. Brian took a break in between and went to PT and I got to see him walk with his right prosthesis. It was good to watch him. His surgery tomorrow is going to be early. They want him there at 5:30. I guess we will be going to bed early tonight. I will let you all know as soon as possible how the surgery went and how he is doing.

I met with some of the other Moms that I became friendly with when I was here before. It was good to see them since we all have a lot in common.

I am going to get a rental car on Wednesday or Thursday, through the Yellow Ribbon Foundation. I won't have to pay for it, not that I plan on driving anywhere too complicated.

I wanted to ask you all to please respect that these are private emails. I don't mind if you share them or forward to someone on your email list, but please don't post them in public forums or bulletin boards. They are private and I know Brian would not like it. Thanks.

I will keep you posted on his surgery tomorrow. Keep him in your prayers.

Love,
Roberta

That last paragraph was directed to someone who had posted my emails on My Space.Com or something like that. I did not want that. Although I was sending these emails to around 35 people, they were my family and my friends. I did not want my emails posted for everyone in the whole world to read. To me they were private.

So why am I writing this account now? I wonder sometimes. I find that it is cathartic for me to write it all down and detail it. I'm trying to "let it go". I'm trying to process it and to accept it. I am having a very hard time with that. I am now seeing a counselor who is helping me with this. Just the act of writing this is bringing tears to my eyes. It doesn't take much anymore. I am angry at what happened to my son. I am angry that it is happening to so many sons and daughters. I am forever grateful that he is alive, and he will never have to go back to Iraq, but I am angry. My heart breaks when I see how he struggles to recover.

I will be driving down the street, listening to the radio. I don't know why this happens, but all of a sudden I am picturing in my mind Brian lying in a hole with his legs all mangled and bloody. I physically become ill and sometimes gag. The tears come. The anguish. I have to learn to overcome this and move on. If Brian can, then so can I. And I will. It is just going to take some time.

So the pre-op red tape. It was awful. Go over to the hospital at a God forsaken early hour to sit there and wait. That was how it was every time he had to have outpatient surgery. I give him all the credit in the world, because I would have lost it long before. It usually involved talking with the anesthesiologist and having blood drawn and being weighed. That's pretty much it. And it took several hours to accomplish this. I guess Brian was used to the Army way, but I certainly was not. I never said anything because I did not want him to become any angrier than he was. It was something that I never quite got used to doing, as many times as we did it.

I was happy to meet up with some of the Moms that were here. Sandy and Faye were my favorite and we seemed to connect with each other from the beginning. Sandy always had a smile on her face and a hug for me. Her son lost one arm and the other was badly injured. Sandy and her husband, Jeff, were there together for a long time. But I think that they started taking turns being there after a while. Faye's son, Nick, hurt his leg badly. He had a couple of surgeries and was struggling with severe pain. Faye knew everything and everybody. She was a source of comfort and strength to me. I miss them both more than I ever realized I would.

Tue, 18 Jul 2006 13:17

Hi all,

The surgery went well this morning. The surgeon said there was no damage to the muscle and it was still intact, so that is great news. He cleaned up the open suture area and re-stitched it. We were back at the hotel room by 11:00am. We have just been resting and figuring out his meds. He has so many it's hard to keep track of them all.

I am going to be getting a rental car tomorrow from the Yellow Ribbon Fund. They will provide one for 28 days at no charge, so that will be great. Not that I know where the hell I can drive to here. *(The Yellow Ribbon Fund was created in early 2005 to assist our injured service members and their families while they recuperate at the Walter Reed Army Medical Center and the National Naval Medical Center. They provide free rental cars, taxi rides, rooms in hotels, tickets to sporting events, concerts, plays, lunches, dinners, golf games, fishing trips, etc. Learn more about them at www.yellowribbonfund.com).*

Yesterday, when we were doing the whole pre-op process, a little kid about three years old walked over to Brian and touched his right stump. Brian didn't say anything, but then neither did the kid's parents. He came back two minutes later and touched it again. This time I pushed his hand away and told him not to touch. Then I glared at his parents. I mean really, who would let their child do that to someone. What if he decided to smack Brian's stump?? You never know what's on the mind of a three year old, or what they are going to do.

It's very hot here, and I hear it's very hot at home. Thank goodness for air conditioning. That's it from Washington. Keep Brian in your prayers. I think he is going to have some pain issues later.

Love,
Roberta

That whole situation with the little boy drove me nuts. His parents were not paying any attention to him. He came over to Brian a couple of times and just stared at him. That was normal and we expect that when we are out in public, especially from little ones. But for him to come over and put his hand on Brian's stump, well that was just too much. Brian didn't say anything but he didn't take his eyes off the boy. I was jumping out of my skin. I was so angry at his parents for not paying attention to him. I wanted to say something but I thought Brian would be upset if I did. I found out later that he would not have had a problem with me going off on those parents. I just don't get how people can be so ignorant. We saw it every time we went somewhere in public. For the most part, you were free of it in the hospital and on the grounds. But once you left the gates you were at the mercy of ignorant people.

Fri, 21 Jul 2006 03:58

Hi All,

Friday morning. Brian is in a formation right now. For the time being he only has to report on Fridays, but eventually they will make him report every morning. This is his first time reporting so I don't know what happens during formation. I guess it's like roll call.

There is always something to do here – an appointment to go to, prescriptions to refill, blood to be drawn, paperwork to fill out, and questions to ask. It's exhausting. I try to take care of the small stuff so he can concentrate on his PT and OT. I have a bunch of stuff to do today and then tonight we are going to the Friday night steak dinner. We haven't made one yet and I am determined to go. It will be good for both of us.

We actually went out last night! We drove to Silver Springs and went to a Macaroni Grill for dinner and then walked around the mall for a little while, and shopped at Borders. It went well and I only had to make one illegal u-turn on the way back.

I think I am going to lay down for a few minutes while he is at formation, take a little "power nap".

Did anyone hear the announcers during Thursday night's Red Sox game talk about Brian? My sister Sue told me that they wished him well recovering from serious injuries he received in Iraq. That was very nice. I wish I could have heard it.

Take care everyone. Keep the prayers coming.

Love,
Roberta

The whole formation thing was ridiculous. For the Army to expect some of these Soldiers to report every day, given their injuries, made me think that they did not have a clue. They did not know how difficult it was for some of them to get to the building where the formations were held. Brian hated going. He was angry that they expected him to go through all that bull to report to formation. I know they wanted to be able to keep track of the Soldiers, but in Brian's mind, where was he going to go? He has no legs. Where was he going to go?

Driving in Washington was not my idea of a good time. I was a wreck every time I pulled out onto Georgia Avenue. The area around Walter Reed was not the best and I was nervous driving there. One time when we were out I slammed the brakes on (a stop sign popped up out of nowhere) and Brian got very angry with me. He said it was the most awful feeling to want to put your feet down to brace yourself and realize you can't. He said it was a very frightening feeling. I tried to be more cautious driving with him in the car. On another occasion, I ran right through a stop sign. I don't know where he got the courage to ride with me. I just felt so out of place driving that rental car in a strange city. Eventually I got much better at it.

Mon, 24 Jul 2006, 12:14

Hi All,

I know it's been a while since I last wrote. It just gets busy here and I tire easily. I have to learn to pace myself. Things are going "wellish". Brian got casted for his left prosthesis today. But he was also told that he probably has an infection at the suture site. He had to go back on Keflex and can't wear his special "sock" on that leg until it clears up. We both have to learn to pace ourselves. He is sleeping right now, he passed out right after lunch. It was a hectic day today.

We did get the rental car, but it is actually very hard for Brian to get in and out of it. It's a Pontiac Sunbird, or Sunfire or some dammed thing, but it's just too small. I'm gong to call the rental place and see if I can get another. Plus, they put the wrong plate number on the rental agreement and the guards at the Forest Glenn PX gave me a hard time about it. Hopefully they will have a larger car that we can use.

We did the Friday night steak dinner that they have every week. Of course, just because I was dying for a nice steak they didn't have it. We went to the Department of Interior building and they had a buffet on the roof top. It was really beautiful but the food was not that great. Next time I am here maybe we can catch it.

Today, Brian and I met President Bush. He came in to PT and met with ten of the patients. You had to be selected to be able to meet him so it was an honor for Brian. I know how some people feel about him, but he is the president. He was very personable with everyone, Soldiers, family and staff. He spent at least five minutes with each patient asking questions about them and their injuries. When he got to us, the woman who introduced us said, "This is Sgt. Brian Fountaine, and this is his wife, Roberta." I quickly corrected her and President Bush laughed. He put his arm around me, and said, "You're the Mom, right?", and then he kissed my head!!!!

Then he shook Brian's hand and sat down beside him and we chatted for quite some time – about Brian, Fort Hood, his injuries and prognosis, the Red Sox, and I forget what else. While there he presented four Purple Hearts to Soldiers who hadn't yet received theirs.

I spoke to the Lieutenant Colonel, whoever, about Brian. He got his Purple Heart in Iraq but doesn't remember getting it. He didn't know he had it until someone pulled it out of his duffel bag in the hospital. Brian wanted the President to present it to him, but apparently that is against the rules. If it was officially presented they can't do it again. He did not get the certificate that comes with it, so the Lieutenant Colonel is going to check into it and find out what happened. Brian was disappointed that the President couldn't present it, but he was glad for the chance to meet him.

I am flying home Wednesday morning. I am looking forward to seeing my family, especially Haley. She is growing like crazy. I haven't seen her in a while. I will be home until August 6. Back to work on Thursday and life goes on. I organized things in his hotel room. It better stay that way while I am gone. Brian's Dad will be here to take over.

That's about it here. The weather is much improved today – very comfortable. I'm actually freezing right now. Brian is always hot so the air conditioner is always on. I will have to go outside to warm up. Take care and please keep him in your prayers.

Love,
Roberta

I was not able to get a bigger car so we would make do with the one we had. It was good to have it though, for doing grocery shopping and errands. We obviously could not "cook" meals in our hotel room at the Mologne House. But we were very sick of eating at the hospital, Subway, the restaurant in the hotel, and Burger King. Those are your options when you are at Walter Reed. Having the car gave us the opportunity to go out to dinner once in a while. We had a small fridge and microwave in the room, so I bought things like salad fixings, canned soups and pastas, cold cuts, and snacks. It wasn't much, but it was something. The restaurant in the hotel specialized in fried everything. The hospital cafeteria specialized in cafeteria food, and Subway and Burger King – well you know what they specialize in. Not the healthiest of diets, but we did the best we could.

It's funny, but back then I was grateful to have a room to be near him. I still am grateful for being able to be with him but I wonder if they could do better in the food department. Especially when you think about the Soldiers recovering from their injuries and how important a good diet is for them. I wonder if that will ever change.

The first Friday night dinner we attended was a bit disappointing to us. The view was beautiful, but it was hot out and Brian was not very comfortable. The food was probably very good, but we were both very disappointed that it wasn't a steak dinner! I have gone to many since that first one and they have all been wonderful. They were the highlight of my weeks there. Brian only went to one other with me, again on the rooftop of a restaurant. It was beautiful and the food was amazing. We could see the planes taking off and landing at Reagan Airport, and the night lights were very pretty.

Brian was bothered by it all though. You could hear sirens in the distance and see lights flashing. I don't know what actually happened but he got very upset. He tried to talk to me about it but he just couldn't. I wasn't sure what to do to help him, but thank goodness there was a man there, a peer counselor at the hospital, and still in the Air Force. He lost a leg. I can't remember his name, or how he lost his leg, but I can still see his face. He saw what was happening to Brian and knew just what to say to him. His wife was very committed to helping wounded warriors as well and was very kind to me. She told me that her husband knew what to do and say to Brian and told me not to worry. He talked Brian through whatever it was that he was going through and helped us to get back to the bus. I'm not sure what we would have done if he wasn't there.

Meeting the President was a strange experience. We had to be cleared to meet him. I guess they probably did a background check on us. You could only meet him if you were on "the list". The morning of his visit we were told to be at the hospital at 8:00am. They were going to shut everything down a few minutes before he arrived and it would stay that way until he left. By shutting down, that meant certain floors of the hospital would be off limits, and certain hallways and elevators. It was a pretty warm day, as most of them were, and we got there a few minutes early.

Someone mentioned that you needed your driver's license because they were checking ID's. At that moment I realized that I had left my license in the rental car. Every time you come onto the post, you have to present your license or military ID to the guards at the gate so I had left my license out in the car. I had to go all the way back to the hotel parking lot to retrieve my license.

By the time I got back to the hospital I was dripping in sweat and my back was killing me. Then I could not find my way back to the PT room. With most of the corridors blocked off, as well as the elevators, I was having a hard time getting back there. I had to show my license to one of the Secret Service men and he checked to make sure I was on the list before they would let me get back to the PT room. There were hospital guards, police, Secret Service, FBI, bomb sniffing dogs, and lots of military big wigs crawling around the whole area in and around

PT. There were also camera people and front people who came around and took all our names and where we lived and the local newspapers so any pictures could be sent to us, and also put in our hometown paper.

Then the President arrived. I had mixed feelings about his visit but I also knew that this was an honor for Brian to meet him. Despite what anyone thinks of him, it is not every day that a person gets to meet the President of the United States of America. I also knew that Brian really wanted the President to present him with his Purple Heart. He was very disappointed when he found out that could not happen. He was actually pretty angry. But he pulled it together and had a good conversation with the President when he came to our table. He is a lot smaller in person than he is on television.

Thu, 27 Jul 2006 09:08

Hi everyone,

Just a quick note to let you know that I'm home. I'm going to try and get some extra rest, but who knows if that will work out.

I talked to Brian last night and he said they are going to x-ray his right leg to see if the bone is growing. It's very weird but the bones will continue to grow even after an amputation. They put him on meds to prevent it, but it doesn't always work. When the bone grows it resembles a head of broccoli – that would obviously be painful with his prosthesis. So they need to keep an eye on that. He sounded good otherwise. He and his Dad were on a mission to find a Wal Mart, although I'm not sure why.

It's good to be home, and be back to work. I work for a very generous company. It just occurred to me that I haven't missed a day's pay since all this happened, and I know I didn't have that much vacation time. I have only been there a year. So, either someone is messing up, or my boss is very generous.

I will keep you all posted on Brian's progress and his adventures. Keep him in your prayers.

Love,
Roberta

I don't think I could every fully describe how tired I was. There were days when I did not think I was capable of walking another step. It was constant walking, pushing, and sometimes running to keep up with him. I would be in tears or huffing and puffing so hard I was afraid I was going to have a heart attack. I never slept as soundly as I did there. I have sleep apnea and I'm sure my snoring didn't help Brian's sleep. He did not sleep well to begin with, between the pain and the nightmares. I felt bad but there was nothing I could do for him. I also had to get some sleep or I would never survive the next day.

As it was, I would often take a nap in the afternoon when all the appointments were done for the day. A couple of times I tried to dole out his meds into one of those weekly containers they have, but I always messed them up. I could not concentrate on them. I could not focus to read the prescription directions. Brian ended up doing it, and it was probably a good thing.

When the weekends came we would venture out to a local mall, or bookstore, but for the most part we would just lie around watching movies. I would read and Brian would play his computer games. Or I would sleep and Brian would play his computer games!!

There was laundry to do although there was never much. Brian mostly wore shorts and t-shirts so it was easy doing his laundry.

Brian and Roberta at their first Friday night dinner

Brian with Paul, his Dad

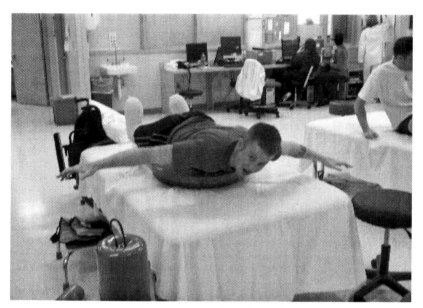

Brian – part of daily PT

MY SON IS ALIVE...

THE MEDIA BLITZ BEGINS

Mon, 31 Jul 2006 04:05

Hi all,

Is it hot enough?? I thought Washington was bad. Not much to report. Brian may get the stitches out today. And he has an appointment with a reporter from the Boston Globe. There was a story about him in the Dorchester Reporter and the Globe picked it up and wants to pursue it.

I'm not sure what is going on with him. He isn't very talkative when I call. I'm going to call his Dad today and see if there is anything wrong. Maybe he just misses his Mom.

Keep cool everyone, and keep Brian in your prayers.

Love,
Roberta

This is when all the media attention began. It started innocently enough with the story in the Dorchester Reporter. The White House photographers sent the picture they took of Brian and me with the President to the Reporter. Brian's home address is listed as his Dad's address in Dorchester. Things just snowballed from there. The Boston Globe, the Bill O'Reilly Show on Fox, it just kept going on and on.

As far as him not being very talkative, I began to realize that he would go through these "spells" frequently. I wanted to believe that he was ok mentally and that he was strong and would survive what happened to him. He will survive but it won't be an easy road for him. The things that he saw in Iraq and the injuries he suffered have left tremendous scars on him physically and mentally. Sometimes he would talk about what happened to him and how he was feeling, but I did not know what to say to him. He wasn't always looking for me to say anything. He just needed someone to listen to what he had to say.

I know he had nightmares that haunted him and I know he was in pain most of the time. I had to accept that I could not "fix" his physical and emotional scars. As a mother I thought that me just being there would be enough – loving him and being there for him. But it wasn't. It helped him to have his Dad and me there, but it was not going to be enough.

Wed, 2 Aug 2006 08:31

Hi Everyone,
The article about Brian is in today's Boston Globe. Thanks, Robin, for sending me that.
I'm having a hard time now. It's hard to read in black and white.

Love,
Roberta

It was very strange and surreal reading about Brian in the Boston Globe. It hurt to see what happened to him in print. It also hurt to see that the reporter who wrote the story took a lot of things out of context. Brian was very angry. He made Brian out to be anti-war and anti-Bush. That is not what he wanted to express or to say. We soon realized that most of the reporters or journalists had their own agendas and didn't much care about Brian personally. It was a hard lesson to learn.

Sun, 6 Aug 2006 06:02

Hi all,
Just a quick email to let you know that I am heading back to DC early Monday morning.
I'm still tired. I guess I will never "catch up" with rest. I don't know what's on the agenda while I am there so I will keep you all posted.

Keep October 1 open for the benefit meat raffle for Brian. I will post more information when I have more details. I am going to try and get some things from the man who runs the Wounded Warrior Program at the hospital – information packets or whatever I can get from him. There is a need for people to know about this great organization.

On a very disturbing note, Brian was told the other day that he may have to take a roommate at the Mologne House. The reason – they are running out of room for the outpatients. That makes me angry and crazy on so many levels. Running out of room? What does that tell you? How many more Soldiers are going to be hurt, disabled, or maimed before this is all over with? Running out of room? It breaks my heart.

Brian won't be taking a roommate as Paul and I are still his non medical attendants so that won't be an issue. He does not want a roommate, for lots of reasons, all of which are legitimate. If he doesn't want a roommate he shouldn't be forced to take one. Not after all he has been through.

Anyway, that's my little rant, and I will stop now. I could go on forever. I will be sending updates from DC. Keep your good thoughts and prayers coming.

Love,
Roberta

It was impossible to get rest while home. There were so many things I needed to catch up on and so little time to do it. Being tired became a way of life for me. It still is.

It broke my heart to see the Soldiers arriving every day or so. They just kept coming. They were running out of room for the outpatients. These wounded warriors needed medical care and were not ready to go home or go back to their units. The amputees needed time to learn how to walk with their prosthetics. There were all kinds of injured Soldiers there. They needed places for them to stay. I spoke to a couple of female Soldiers who were sharing a hotel room at the Mologne House. They did not have a choice and accepted the situation.

I did not know about Building 18. I hadn't heard any rumors or talk about it until that story broke in the Washington Post.

Mon, 7 Aug 2006 16:01

Hi Everyone,

Got here safely. Brian is doing well. He had a great visit with his friend and they had a fun weekend.

I can't remember if I told you about the article in the Boston Herald. That came out today. It has a few inaccuracies in it but not a bad article altogether.

Brian has surgery this week to remove the filter that they placed in his artery for the blood clot. It should be a simple procedure. He is using crutches now in PT and that's pretty cool. He still can't wear a left prosthetic as there remains a bit of infected area. It's clearing but they want it to heal completely. He doesn't get OT now, not until he has both prosthetics in place. So it's pretty much just PT for him. He is going to start using the pool here at the hospital also. He is going to be learning how to kayak. They do that here in the PT pool. He has to learn how to tip over and right himself in the kayak. I don't think I will be watching him do that. It will make me too nervous.

I ran into one of the Moms that I have become friendly with and she looks rough. She hasn't been able to leave to go home for a break and looks completely exhausted and stressed out. I feel so bad for her. We talked for a long time and maybe that helped her a little. I hope so, she is a sweet woman.

That's it for now. I will keep you posted. Take care everyone and keep Brian in your prayers. Thanks.

Love,
Roberta

I was always so happy to be back. I missed Brian terribly when I went back home. And I worried about him. I guess I will always worry about him. It's my job, and I'm very good at it!

Tue, 8 Aug 2006 13:34

Hi all,

It seems that Brian has become quite the news story. The woman from the Herald wants to come down and interview him again. CBS news in Boston called and did a phone interview, and at 5:20 this afternoon we are getting picked up by a limo and driven to a DC news station so he can do an interview with Bill O'Rielly from the Fox Channel (where he corrected the erroneous statements made in the Boston Globe story). That show airs at 8:00 pm and I think again at 11:00 pm. I hope it goes well. I don't trust some of the media as far as I can see them. They have their own agendas.

He has surgery tomorrow to remove the filter and that should be it for surgeries. Yeah! Now if the left stump would just heal. Patience…

Keep him in your prayers.

Love,
Roberta

Wed, 9 Aug 2006 17:35

Hi Everyone,

Brian's surgery went well. He was out of it most of the day today. His neck is a little sore from them going through a neck artery to remove the blood clot filter, but he is doing well physically. He is angry today, at the world and at everyone. I find it best to just leave him alone when he is like this.

I met a little five month old boy today. He was with his grandma while his parents were taking a nap. The boy has glaucoma in both his eyes. He had surgery the other day and they don't think it worked. The pressure in his eyes went up again today. He is the cutest little thing. He smiled at me and made my day. His parents are in the Air Force, stationed in Germany, but they don't have any pediatric ophthalmologists' there so they sent him here for his surgery. I got the impression from his grandma that he would probably be blind soon unless they can do something else to help him.

It is heartbreaking here – and exhausting. So say a prayer for the little boy. I'm going to get to bed, will post again in a couple of days.

Love,
Roberta

I'm not sure why but Brian was impossible to be with. He was hurting and angry and just as miserable as he could be. I could not blame him and, before we ended up saying things we didn't mean to each other, I decided to leave. I made sure he had everything he needed and then I just prowled the halls, the lobby, and the back courtyard of the hotel. I checked on him from time to time to make sure he was ok, but I knew he just wanted to be left alone.

In my "prowling", I met a lot of people. I saw a lot and I heard a lot. I met another sweet baby whose parents were stationed in Germany. He also had a complicated medical condition that the hospitals in Germany could not handle. I don't know how these young parents handled the stress. Their entire lives were uprooted and their child's health and well being was precarious. I guess they just did what they had to do, just like I was doing.

Sat, 12 Aug 2006 06:44

Hi Everyone,

It's been a few days but I've been busy. Brian started feeling sick Thursday afternoon. He had the cold sweats alternating with feeling feverish, was nauseous and had a vicious headache. Friday morning he wasn't up for reporting to formation so he called his Sergeant, who gave him a hard time. He wanted to try going to PT, so we did, but that didn't work either. He ended up lying in one of the rooms with the lights out for a couple of hours.

While he was doing that, I was trying to get some prescriptions refilled. I had to wait just like everyone else, so it took me over an hour to pick up that script. Then his sergeant wanted a note from a doctor saying why he missed formation so I had to deal with that. They think because he missed some doses of certain meds when he had his neck surgery, it made him sick. I don't think that is it though because he still felt sick last night. He actually threw up and felt better afterwards. When I woke up this morning the bucket was beside his bed again.

He is still sleeping right now. If he is still sick today I will take him to the ER. I know he won't like it but he will have to get over it.

Early Friday around 4:00 am we were awakened by some type of domestic brawl in the hallway outside our room. The police had to come and deal with it. Needless to say, we both have had it here in the Mologne House. We are now dealing with bugs in the room and I can't cope with that. I am now having nightmares about bugs and being out in the hallway spraying bratty children with bug spray.

So on Friday morning, among all the other things I did, I had Brian's social worker put us in to move to the Fisher House. It's a family oriented place with a large common kitchen fully equipped for cooking, a dining area, living room, and family room. You have your own bedroom and bath similar to a hotel set up. We would still share a bedroom with twin beds, but that's what we do here. There is a nice patio area outside and it's supposed to be so much better. There is no maid service but we can cope with that.

After what the maids did to Brian at the beginning of the week we really don't care. They threw away a box that had all the cards that people have sent him. It was sitting there for three weeks and, all of a sudden, they decided it was trash. We tried to get them back but it was too late.

Last night he insisted that I go to the Friday Night Dinner. I am glad I did because I had a good time. I have made some friends here and they were both there. I met some new friends as well. The dinner was at the Capitol Club, a very "hoity toity" place. They had a private room set up for us with appetizers of all sorts. The dinner was filet mignon, mashed potatoes, and broccoli. It was yummy. They had an open bar as well. They gave us goody bags and door prizes and it was just a real fun time. The stories I could tell you about some of the families that are here – some are tragic, some heroic, and some comic. It is an amazing experience to go through. (The Friday Night Dinners are made possible by the Aleethia Foundation. Their mission is to support the newly injured troops with short-term therapeutic recreation. The doctors have determined that it is beneficial for the newly injured troops to get out of the hospital environment occasionally. Their mission is to help them get out for meals, movies, sightseeing, and visits to interesting sites. Their main focus is the Friday Night Dinners for the wounded troops from Walter Reed Army Medical Center and National Naval Medical Center. To make a donation or to learn more about this fabulous organization, go to www.aleethia.org)

I guess I have rambled enough. Brian is still sleeping despite my clickety clack on the keyboard. Depending on how he is feeling, I want to get him out today to do a little shopping or something fun. It all depends on how he is feeling.

I hope all is well with all of you. I hope you realize that sending these emails to you is like medicine for me. It helps me to feel connected to home and family and friends. So thank you for helping me stay connected.

Keep Brian in your prayers.

Love,
Roberta

I don't think I have ever seen Brian look so sick. He was making me nervous but Carrie, his therapist, thought he was going to be ok. The pain he was having was like a migraine. He was really in rough shape and all I wanted to do was get him back to the hotel room so he could lay in the dark and be as cool and comfortable as possible.

I was having one of those moments where frustration and anger gave way to tears. But that can be effective when you are trying to get a point across to someone. That someone was Brian's social worker. He clearly saw that I was at my wit's end as far as the hotel was concerned. I told him about the cockroaches that I had seen in the lobby and in our room, the drunken brawl in the hallway, and everything else that I could think of. It's not that it was a bad place, it just wasn't the place for us. I know bugs are everywhere and you do what you can to keep them out, but that doesn't mean I was happy about seeing them in our room.

I was very reluctant to leave him alone that night and go to the Friday night dinner. He still wasn't feeling well although he looked a bit better after sleeping for a couple of hours. He insisted that I go so I decided that I would. I'm very glad that I did because I ended up having so much fun and just laughing a lot. It made me feel more "normal" again. I felt like the old Roberta who loved to laugh and have a good time.

I had been so worried about my son that I could barely focus on anything else. I did not like who I had become but I was powerless to do anything about it. One minute I was functioning and doing what I need to do for Brian and the next I was a weepy mess. So going to the dinner was really a good thing. I am glad that I listened to Brian.

Sun, 13 Aug 2006 18:11

Hi all,

Just a quick update to let you know that Brian is feeling much, much better. He actually felt good enough to go out yesterday for a couple of hours to the local mall. He is shopping for things that he needs to take with him on the white water rafting trip that is coming up. And yes, I am going to be insane with worry when he goes, but who am I to try and stop him.

We went back out today. It gets easier and easier with time for both of us – him transferring from the wheel chair to the car and me putting the wheelchair in the trunk.

I don't know if I told you or not, but Brian has been taking an art class offered in occupational therapy. He did a beautiful watercolor that he thinks is awful. I managed to convince him to give it to me. I will cherish this painting always. He has a God given talent with art, something I certainly don't have.

Another week here at Walter Reed. You never know what each day will bring. I have met some amazing people and have seen some amazing things. I am glad that Brian is here and not at another facility.

Keep Brian in your prayers and please say an extra one that we get into the Fisher House soon. Thanks.

Love,
Roberta

Water color Brian painted in occupational therapy

More PT for Brian...

...followed by a field trip to a DC area monument

MY SON IS ALIVE...

BRIAN WALKS!

Mon, 14 Aug 2006 10:41

Hi all,

I have the most awesome news!! My son, after only two months and two days walked today!!! He got both prosthetics on and walked from PT all the way to the prosthetic lab, about 200 feet. It was truly an amazing sight. Brian was very excited but didn't want to show it. I knew he was so proud and so happy to be "standing tall" again. Speaking of which, he is 72" tall now. They may shorten him a little with the prosthetics but we will see. I can't tell you how proud and amazed and in awe I was of him and for him. The whole PT clinic came over to watch him and a bunch of them took pictures. I, of course, left my camera at the hotel but I will take pictures tomorrow for sure.

There will be no stopping him now. They recast his left leg after PT. The swelling is almost gone so he will be more comfortable in the new cap. He has a lot of hard work ahead of him but I know he will meet it head on and with everything he has.

Thank you all for your thoughts and prayers. I know they have helped both of us get through this.

Love,
Roberta

Of course I cried. I was so happy to see him standing. He was so happy. I cried for joy and I cried in sorrow. It's hard to explain but I did that a lot. I had so many conflicting emotions that I tried to hide from Brian. I was thrilled to see him standing, yet at the same time, my heart was broken to see him standing with prosthetics. It was still too fresh in my mind – the explosion and the aftermath. The dammed war and the grief, sorrow, and anguish it caused. He was supposed to be in his tank, dammit, not in a humvee. I still picture his feet in my mind and I remember exactly what they looked like. They were taken from him in a horrible, violent explosion. An explosion that was meant to kill him. He will never see those feet again, never feel the sand between his toes at the beach, never feel them being tickled, or the soft cushion of green grass. He will never again feel that feeling when you stretch and wiggle your toes.

I know there are worse things in life that people suffer through, but to me, this was pretty bad. My handsome, beautiful son. He is still handsome and still beautiful, he just doesn't have any feet. He will stand tall again. I know that in my heart. It won't be easy getting there, but he will.

Wed, 16 Aug 2006 19:45

Hi all,

I just wanted to send this picture of Brian walking today. It was a crazy day with lots of running around and they had to adjust his new left leg a couple of times. He looked very good when he finally got to walk on the new leg. And when his left leg heals completely, he will go places!!

Crazy things are happening and I will post more tomorrow hopefully. I have a lot more to do tomorrow. Army business. Hurry up and wait. That's the Army motto.

Hugs and Love to All,
Roberta

Thu, 17 Aug 2006 15:07

Hi everyone,

It's been an exhausting and crazy couple of days here at Walter Reed. Brian walked outside today with crutches. He did so good it was amazing. He walked on a sloped walkway, on lawn, and on steps, and did so good with all of it. It's hard to get him to stop or slow down, but his therapist Carrie is with him all the way and she knows how to handle him. He also interviewed for a therapy dog today. There is an organization in western Massachusetts that came out to interview him and a couple of other guys. They are thrilled to have someone from Massachusetts to give a dog to. A therapy dog will be Brian's crutches should something happen to his legs. They can also fetch things that he drops, help him get up, and do all sorts of things. Brian loves dogs so he can't wait to get one. It won't be for a while though.

Last night, Brian got invited to go to the Red Sox game Monday against the Yankees. He will be an "honored guest" of the Red Sox. How cool is that! They gave him two extra tickets. I feel bad because he wanted his sister to come with us. His Dad and I are going to go. They are flying him to Boston and will have someone pick him up at the airport and bring him to Fenway Park. I am flying home Sunday morning. Paul and I will just meet him there. They told him he would have box seats but didn't tell him where they would be. There is a slight possibility that he will throw out the first pitch but we aren't sure yet.

He has such a busy schedule. I worry that it's too much. Tomorrow he goes kayaking from 9:00 am to 2:00 pm. Then at 3:00 pm we have the White House tour that we were specially invited to, and then after that is the Friday night dinner. Monday is the game and Tuesday he leaves for the Colorado River white water rafting trip, which will include two days in Vegas. So on Saturday I have to take him to get the last minute stuff for the trip. I have expressed my concerns to all of his therapists and doctors and they tell me not to worry. Not to worry, hah! Who do they think they are dealing with here? I am the queen of worry – not to worry, yeah right!!

There are a couple of fund raisers coming up in the near future. One is at Florian Hall in Dorchester, the Fire Department is sponsoring that one on September 17. Brian will be home for that on a four day pass. The other is the meat raffle at the VFW in Whitman on October 1. The Whitman Legion and the VFW are sponsoring that. Brian will be home for that one as well, for at least two weeks.

My friend Faye and her son Nick are going home tomorrow for Nick's 30 day convalescent leave. I will miss her when I come back. She helps so many people besides taking care of her son. Nick is a National Guard Soldier and was in Iraq when his vehicle got hit by an IED. He has badly damaged legs, one that may never work right again. He's a funny kid who does a great impression of Adam Sandler and makes us all laugh.

That's about it here. Sorry this is so long. I am looking forward to going home. I'm not sure how my boss is going to feel about me not coming to work on Monday. I work for the rest of the week and the following week Chet and I are going to Pennsylvania to visit his daughter, Terri, her husband, Jon, and to meet his two granddaughters that he has yet to see. We will spend four or five days with them and then drive to DC to see Brian for a couple of days. He will be back from his trip by then. Paul will then come in on Monday to stay with him and I am going to be home for a while.

So thank you all again for your prayers. I believe in my heart that they have helped my son.

Love,
Roberta

It was a beautiful sight to see him walking outside. He did not want to go back in. Thank God for Carrie. She knew how to handle her "guys". I was very worried about the pace he was trying to keep. It was exhausting just making the daily trip to the hospital. Sometimes we took the bus but most of the time I would push him about halfway and he would do the rest while I struggled to keep up with him. It would take almost a half hour for my pounding heart to quiet down after that trip, and I would be sweating like crazy.

It's a good thing I gave up smoking a year ago! Brian did not like me worrying about him and he definitely did not like it if I tried to get him to slow down. He was on a roll (pardon the expression), and he did not want to stop.

Sun, 20 Aug 2006 17:21

Hi everyone,
It's been a crazy couple of days, as usual. I'm home now and very glad to be here. I need to recharge my batteries.
On Friday, Brian went kayaking in the morning. They were supposed to be home by 2:00 pm so we could do the tour of the White House. Well, they were all having such a great time kayaking that they didn't get back until just before 3:00 pm. We were all trying to urge Brian to hurry and change – he was still wet from the river. He wanted to shower and there wasn't enough time, so he said forget it, he wasn't going to go. I said fine, but I am going. He went into the hotel and I got on the bus. About ten minutes later we were still sitting there waiting to load everyone and someone told me to look out the window.
There was Brian, WALKING out of the hotel on his two prosthetics and using his crutches! It was an amazing sight. Everyone was watching him and he "walked so tall" to the bus and got on by himself. He did not last long wearing the legs because the left one is still healing, but it was an amazing sight.
We are going to the Red Sox game tomorrow. It should be a fun day. Then on Tuesday he goes for his trip. I worry about that, but I have to learn to give it up to God. He will be fine, right?
The game is at 1:00, so if you can, try to watch it. I don't know where we will be sitting. We will find out when we get there.
"There's no place like home."

Love,
Roberta

I will never forget the sight of him walking out of the hotel on his new "legs". It was amazing. Everyone was watching him and you could feel that they were quietly cheering him on.

I was so happy to be home. I was so exhausted and thought I would get some rest while home. I was wrong about that though. There was always so much for me to catch up on.

BRIAN WALKS!

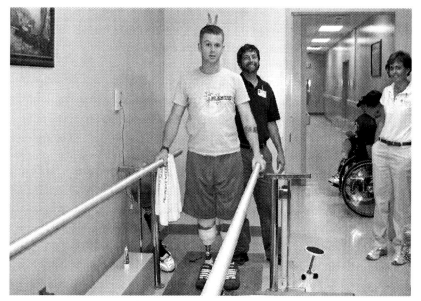

Brian Walks! His therapists are proud of him.

First walking adventure on steps - near the cannon at Walter Reed

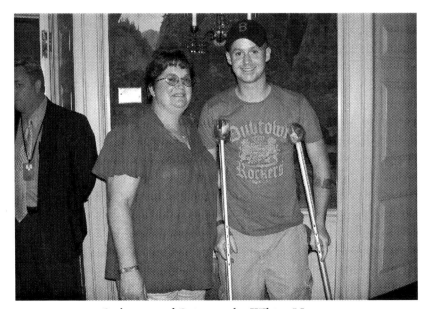

Roberta and Brian at the White House

Worn out after the White House trip – it was a long day

RED SOX AND COLORADO RIVER TRIPS

Tue, 22 Aug 2006 18:16

Hi all,

My first day back at work and it is crazy there. We got bought out by another huge company. There are many changes going on, including some getting fired. It's very interesting now. The new computer system is a nightmare.

Brian's trip to Boston yesterday was sponsored by the Disabled Sports America organization. They do great work with disabled people. They are heavily involved with wounded Soldiers now and want to do whatever they can for them. They paid to fly Brian here and for the ticket. Paul and I met Brian at the airport and then we all took a van to Fenway Park. When we got there, one of the Red Sox PR people had us wait in a hallway while she did some stuff. Brian and Paul practiced throwing the baseball – Brian was very nervous about "making a fool of himself" throwing out the first pitch.

He did great, it was a strike right down the middle of the plate!! It was funny, when we walked onto the field we entered just after the dugout and walked in front of it. I didn't even notice it. I was in awe just being on the field at Fenway Park. I was also nervous for Brian. The game was good even though they lost. Brian really had a great time. His Aunt Robin and Cousin Justin got tickets from a local radio station and he was thrilled to see both of them. That was a totally unexpected surprise for all.

After the game we went out to meet the van and it wasn't there. One of the guys called and the driver said he was stuck in traffic and would not be there for an hour. So Kirk, the man that accompanied Brian from DC, an amputee from the Vietnam War, went over to a limo that was sitting at a set of lights. I don't know what he said to him but the next thing I know we are all piling into the limo and having some cold beers and champagne. It was the strangest thing, but lots of fun! The limo took us to a fancy restaurant where we had a great meal. All in all, it was a great day and we had a great time.

Now he is off to go white water rafting on the Colorado River for ten days. I worry about him but I know they will take good care of him. Chet and I are leaving Sunday morning for our vacation. We are going to visit Chet's daughter and then maybe spend a day or two with Brian. It will be nice to have some alone time with Chet. I just hope the house is in one piece when we get home.

There are a lot of fund raisers coming up and people and organizations are calling me all the time to offer to help raise money. It really is amazing, the support and help from one and all.

Keep him in your thought and prayers while he is away. Thank you all for your support. I really think it is what gets me through all of this.

Love,
Roberta

It was very strange to think about the fund raisers. I had attended many before but having one for your son's benefit was just a weird feeling. Brian was not very comfortable with it either. He did not think that he needed anyone's help. He was wrong but he did not know that. None of us know what the future will hold for him. We like to think that he will be fine and live a happy wonderful life, but we don't know. We don't know what the future holds for any of us. Brian has a lot of obstacles in front of him. I know that he is strong, that he will survive and make a life for himself. But he may need some help along the way. These benefits will provide the financial help that he may need.

The Colorado River white water rafting trip was not what I thought was in Brian's best interest. I did talk with him and he let me know that he really needed to do it., not so much to prove that he could physically but more for a mental relief. He needed to get away from the hospital environment and, I think, also to get away from his Dad and me. I don't know how Paul was when he was there, but I tended to hover. I tried not to, but it was hard. I kept thinking that he should not have to do anything after all he had been through, but of course that was totally the wrong way to be thinking. It was not the way Brian was thinking either. He is stubborn, and independent, and does not like to have people waiting on him.

I also know that a lot of people think that going on the trip was the beginning of a lot of problems Brian soon began to encounter. The trip did more good than harm, despite what challenges came up. Chet and I were at the Mologne House the day he came back from the trip. Although he was tired and dirty looking, he had a new sense of strength that I had not seen before. That was worth whatever price he had to pay. He needed that boost.

Fri, 25 Aug 2006 14:44

Hi all,

Boy, am I glad this week is over. It was absolutely crazy at work. Since our company got bought out by a bigger company, we all had to take drug tests this week. I heard today that 12 people failed. No notice was given for the test. I wonder what is going to happen??

Chet and I are leaving Sunday morning very early to drive to Pennsylvania to visit his daughter. We are both looking forward to this trip very much.

Speaking of Brian, I haven't heard a word from him, so I am thinking that no news is good news! I hope he is having a great time.

Well that's about it for now. I will give you all a break from me and my crazy rambling. Have a great week and I hope to see you all soon.

Love,
Roberta

Fri, 1 Sept 2006 16:46

Hi everyone,

Chet and I drove to DC yesterday. We had a wonderful visit with Chet's daughter, Terri. Her husband, Jon, was the greatest host and took us to some really beautiful places. Their daughters, Kaylinn and Carissa, are beautiful girls that Chet and I fell in love with, and they with us. It was a special visit and I know we will be going back again very soon. Thank you, Terri, for a great visit!!

Brian came in last night from his rafting trip. He was pretty tired but had a wonderful time. He enjoyed the rafting, slept under the stars, and just had a great time. He spent two nights in Vegas and won a little money playing blackjack.

He was a little put out with me because I made him go to the hospital this morning to have his left leg looked at. It was pretty red and oozing quite a bit. They put him on antibiotics and he has to have an MRI done sometime this weekend. They just want to make sure that the infection hasn't gone to his bone.

Then after the hospital we took him to a mall. He had us running around all over the mall, a very big mall. Chet is exhausted and now knows what I go through when I am here. The hospital itself is very big and it's always a long walk to wherever you need to go. Brian's new girlfriend, Mary, is coming in for the long weekend. He is pretty happy about that. Chet and I will head back home tomorrow. I wanted to stop either in Atlantic City or the Jersey Shore somewhere, but I don't think the weather will be good anywhere this weekend. We are getting pounded with Hurricane Ernesto's rain and wind right now.

I miss the Jacuzzi. I am glad the cooler weather is coming. Cassie told me work is getting interesting – new rules, and a few people flunked the surprise drug test that the new company made us all do. Always interesting. (Cassie works at the same place I do).

I hope all is well with everyone. Keep Brian in your prayers. He is upset that his left leg is not healing but he has been very busy lately. He just needs to focus on healing and walking. He got some bad news from some of his fellow Soldiers that are still in Iraq. He still wishes he were there fighting alongside all of them.

Have a great Labor Day Weekend.

Love,
Roberta

Have a great Labor Day Weekend. How dumb it was of me to say that. Brian's left leg was in the beginning stages of what turned out to be a serious infection. It put him through the ringer, and made him miserable. As I write this, ten months have gone by since then, and he was just now declared "free" of infection in his bone on the left leg. Ten months of pure hell with that leg. Worry about losing his knee because of the infection – and frustration. Frustration at not being able to wear his left prosthetic. He had to go on IV antibiotic therapy for a month. He had a couple of "cut downs" just trying to rid his leg of the infection. Thank God he was able to keep his knee. That would have been difficult for him had he lost the left knee – difficult to walk without the knee, and emotionally, to lose more of his body. I cannot begin to imagine what that must have been like for him.

So let me tell you about Mary. They met playing a computer game on line a couple of years ago. They developed a "pen pal" type relationship and enjoyed playing a game (I cannot remember the name). Something like World of Warcraft or something like that. Anyway, I guess they both considered a relationship between them, but because Brian was in the Army, and she lived in Kansas, they both did not think it was a good idea. When Mary found out Brian was injured, she made plans to visit him in DC. It was pretty much love at first sight, and the next thing you know, Mary decided to give up her life in Kansas and move to DC to be with Brian. The first time I met her was her first visit to Brian at the Mologne House. She was with two friends and they only spent a couple of hours visiting. I immediately liked her. The way she talked, her personality, and there was just a "way" about her that let me know she was a strong, capable young woman. I still feel that way about her. She has to be to put up with Brian's shenanigans!

Wed, 6 Sep 2006 04:24

Hi all,

I talked with Brian late last night on the computer. I had a feeling that something wasn't right. He has to have surgery on his left leg again. It is infected and they need to see if it has gone to the bone. If it has they will have to take more of his left leg off. The part that I don't get is that they aren't doing the surgery until the 14th. The surgeon is booked solid so I would have to assume that it is ok to wait till then. I just wish they would do it now. I hate the waiting. Brian, needless to say, is upset and blames himself for this. Between the wheelchair accident and going to the Colorado River, he says he has no one to blame but himself. If they take any more of his left leg off, he will have a much harder time learning to walk, and his gait will be affected.

I don't know if his leaves will be affected by this also. I hope not.

That's it for now. I will keep you posted. Needless to say, keep him in your prayers.

Love,
Roberta

First pitch at Red Sox game – a strike down the middle
Paul, his dad, and Carolyn Hall, proudly look on

A great thrill for two lifelong Red Sox fans

MY SON IS ALIVE...

CONTINUING CHALLENGES – AND A FUND RAISER

Tue, 12 Sep 2006 11:43

Hi everyone,

I just got off the phone with Paul. He told me they postponed Brian's surgery to the 25th of this month. I don't know why, other than Brian's doctor will not be available until then. I asked Paul if he has looked at Brian's left leg and he said it looks pretty good. The redness is going away and it's starting to close again. I think they may not have to do it at all if it looks good by then. They obviously are not too concerned about it.

Brian is supposed to come home this weekend for the Boston Fire Dept fund raiser. That's on Sunday at 4:00 pm at Florian Hall in Dorchester if anyone wants to go. It will be a silent auction and raffles of gift certificates. Some of them are pretty nice. There won't be any food there, at least that is what I was told. Brian is flying in on Friday or Saturday. Paul is going to let me know as soon as he finds out. He will be staying with Paul this weekend. I think he goes back to DC on Wednesday.

I will be going back with him for my ten day stretch. I may stay a bit longer this time as well. We will see. It should be my last time going down there except when I go for weekend visits. Brian's girlfriend, Mary, is moving to DC from Kansas. She wants to be with him and help him recover. And of course, he would rather she be there instead of his Mom or Dad! I don't know what his plans are while he is home. We are just trying to get through this fund raiser on Sunday. It is supposed to be "very well attended".

Yesterday was a tough day. I remember where I was five years ago when the planes hit the Twin Towers. Brian was home on leave, just graduated from boot camp. He was recruiting at the high school to get extra leave time. A couple of hours after it happened I went to the high school to find him. I just wrapped my arms around him and cried. I knew then, because of that terrible act of terrorism, that Brian would go somewhere bad. I didn't imagine something bad would happen, but I knew it was a possibility. Little did I know. He is alive though, and for that I will always be grateful.

Sorry to ramble. I hope all is well with everyone. I thank you for your prayers and thoughts.

Love,
Roberta

Tue, 19 Sep 2006 04:23

Hi all,

I wrote an email last night and when I hit the send button, I got, "There was a problem". I came very close to tossing the computer out the window.

It's been an emotional couple of days for all of us. Brian came in on Saturday and was greeted by the Boston and Massport Fire Departments. Then Sunday was the fund raiser that the Boston Fire Department held for him. It was very well attended and quite a success. Brian was overwhelmed and emotional. He was interviewed by a few TV stations and newspapers. I think some of you probably saw him on the news.

He is having a hard time right now. He is suffering with exhaustion, the left leg infections, depression, and guilt. Survivor's guilt. He lost some men from his unit to the war and he is questioning why he is still here and they are not. I don't know what to do to help him except to just be there if he needs me. And to feed him some home cooking, of course!

He goes back to DC tomorrow. We have different flights and airlines but will arrive in DC at pretty much the same time. It will be an interesting arrival trying to coordinate the ride to Walter Reed. Brian told me last night that this will be the last time for me and his Dad going to DC. He wants to have some alone time before Mary gets there. I have to respect his wishes but I will worry about him. I am hoping we can get into the Fisher House while I am there. That will be a big help for him.

I have to get to work. They have been patient with me and very good by paying me through all of this, but with the new owners, I don't know how they will feel about me going away.

Please keep Brian in your prayers.

Love,
Roberta

The fund raiser was amazing. There were so many people there, all there for Brian. The room where they held the silent auction was so crowded you could barely move. Brian spoke to the audience and was very uplifting and very emotional. He stayed for a couple of hours but was so exhausted he ended up going back to Paul's to get some rest. The Fire Department raised so much money for him, it was amazing. It was also very nice to see a lot of the guys on the job that I have known since Paul started work there.

Thu, 21 Sep 2006 18:36

Hi all,

We both had a good flight to DC yesterday. Brian got his wallet back that he lost on the trip to Boston. Some kind woman found it and turned it into the airlines so we picked it up when we got back here.

He had physical therapy this morning and went to occupational therapy for his painting class. He was pretty tired after the weekend home so we just stayed in the hotel room all day. He has set up an area in the room for painting and doing models and that sort of thing. It's good therapy for him and he loves doing it.

He will be having surgery on Monday to remove another inch of so of his left leg. They feel that the infection may be in the bone so they are going to take some off to be safe. The leg will never heal the way it is right now, so the surgery will help. He is going to be inpatient with this surgery for a couple of days at least. He is disappointed but also feels like this is it. When this surgery is over, he will be taking a step forward, so to speak – a step to being able to use both prosthetics. Something he had a taste of and wants again badly.

He will not come home for the October 1st fundraiser. The trip home this past weekend was too much for him, as was the rafting trip. He knows that now and regrets doing it, but that is in the past. What's done is done. With surgery on Monday, it is just too much for him.

I have to tell you that there is nothing more heart wrenching than the sight of your son getting out of a car at your home and "walking" on his knees to get into your house. My heart broke when I saw that. I have to get my house adapted for him as soon as possible. He is coming home for Thanksgiving and I want him to be able to come into my home with some dignity, either with his wheelchair, or with his new legs. That is my goal and I will make it happen, one way or the other.

We are getting ready for bed. He has formation in the morning so we have to get up early.

Please keep him in your prayers. He needs them.

Love,
Roberta

I still can't think about him crawling up the walkway without tears coming. I felt so bad for him, like I had let him down. I know he did not think that way but I also know it was hard for him to come into my house like that. We still have things to do to the house to make it more comfortable for him when he is here. I will make that happen, no matter what.

Earlier, the Junior Vice Commander from the Hanson American Legion Post came to see me. He asked about Brian and wanted to know what they could do for us. At first I told him there was nothing but then I decided to just suck it up and I told him that we needed help making the front door large enough for a wheelchair, a portable handicap ramp, and to remove the hearth in the living room. The wheelchair cannot get around it. When Brian is here for his pass and convalescence leave, I want him to be able to come into my house. This will help. Gordon told me to consider it done. It will be a great help if they do this for us. We don't have the extra cash right now and neither one of us is very handy.

It was very difficult for me to ask for help. It still is, but I have gotten better at it. The American Legion in Hanson really came through for us. The ramp got built, the hearth removed, and the door was widened so his wheelchair would fit through. With the help of the Legion, and the Veteran's Agent in Hanson, these amazing things got done to help Brian move around when he was home.

Mon, 25 Sep 2006 04:02

Hi all,

I just wanted to ask you all to say a prayer this morning for Brian. He has surgery at 8:00am to cut his left leg down a couple of inches to get rid of the infection once and for all. This is to get rid of the infection once and for all. Hopefully they won't have to go above the knee.

I will post later about how his surgery went. Thanks for the prayers.

Love,
Roberta

Mon, 25 Sep 2006 17:34

Hi All,

Brian did well with surgery today. He had to be there at 8:00 am, but they didn't actually do the surgery until a little past noon. Poor guy. It went well and the doctor was pleased. They took almost an inch off his left leg and there was plenty of good muscle to wrap around the bone. That is good. It's just after 8:00 pm and I just got back to the hotel. He is resting, a bit irritable, but otherwise ok. They still have the spinal block in him. I don't know when they will take that out but he feels nothing from his waist down. He is mad because he can't get his laptop working, there's not a good connection in the room he is in. I actually had to go out and get him some food for supper. There isn't any room in Ward 57 for him, so they put him in Ward 66, a short stay unit. They don't serve food there.

I managed to get some stuff done while at the hospital and I also started hounding his social worker about the Fisher Hose. I'm getting angry because people who live there keep telling me that families have moved out, but no one calls us to move in. I am thinking that you have to have connections to get in there. I don't know what else it could be. I plan on hounding him until we get in there.

I am coming home on Saturday. Brian will definitely not be coming for the fund raiser at the VFW. He will not be up for it. His surgeon doesn't want him doing anything for a long time. He and I spoke to Harvey, the head of OT, and told him to stop pushing Brian to go on trips. No more trips until he is completely healed. He will have the rest of his life to go on whatever trips he chooses. They sort of push the guys to go on these trips. They believe it is good for their morale, and they are right, but some just aren't ready for it. And they hate to admit to it. I talked today with a young man who lost his arm, and he said after PT and OT he is too damned tired to do anything else. He said he needed his rest more than he needed to have fun right now. I agree.

I met Bo Derek and John Corbett today at PT. I was getting Brian's wheelchair fixed and they were there visiting Soldiers. Some of you may not know who Bo Derek is, and it's kind of hard to explain, but she is the tiniest bit of a thing in person. She is very involved in adaptive sporting events like skiing. John Corbett played the sexy DJ on Northern Exposure and of late was a love interest to the main character on "Sex in the City". They were both very nice, and he is just as sexy in person as he is on TV.

Paul is coming in on Saturday to be with Brian until Mary gets here. I hope the two of them can figure out how to get along. They have been butting heads lately. Father/son stuff I guess.

That's it here. I hope to see a lot of you on Sunday, October 1 at 1:00 pm at the Whitman VFW on Essex Street. Brian will be there in spirit and I will be there to hug you all for keeping him in your prayers. He never would have come this far without them.

Love,
Roberta

John Gonsalves, founder of "Homes for our Troops" at fund raiser the Boston Fire Department held for Brian

Brian with some of his high school friends – at the Boston Fire Department fund raiser

Brian and Mary

Brian and Mary

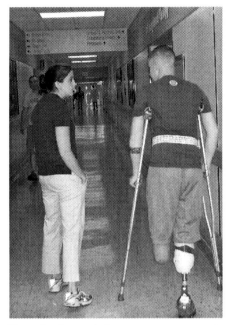

Carrie, Brian's physical therapist, encouraging Brian

FISHER HOUSE AND ANOTHER FUND RAISER

Tue, 26 Sep 2006 15:49

Hi all,

Pretty amazing huh!!! I am typing this from our room at the Fisher House. I got a call this morning and it's been a whirlwind and exhausting day. I spent the entire day moving. I can't believe how much stuff we have acquired in the short time we have been here. I had little to no help and I am beyond tired. But we are here and I will post more about our new living space in a day or two. I'm just too tired. I only saw Brian this morning and he was in considerable pain. We got them to change his pain meds and I put up a fuss about his room. He got sent to the fifth floor this morning and they will take better care of him. He is frustrated because he has no reception on his cell and can't get the laptop to work. I told him to suck it up. He has to stay there for a couple of days and then it's nothing but going up from there on.

I'm going to go eat. I haven't had a thing since breakfast, and then I will putter in the room for a while and go to bed. Your thoughts and prayers must have worked and I thank you all for them. There are some familiar faces here and it's good to see them. Details later.

Love,
Roberta

It was the most exhausting day I had ever gone through. I made so many trips from the room to the hotel lobby with all of our stuff, using the luggage carts, I lost count. The hotel had the van drivers load my stuff in one of the vans and they brought it over to the Fisher House for me. Then I had to unload the van and unpack. The Fisher House is beautiful and I was so happy to be there, I didn't care what it took to get there. I knew Brian and Mary would be much happier there.

Wed, 27 Sep 2006 17:07

Hi everyone,

Well, I had a rough night at the Fisher House, but it is still worth it being here. The people in the room next door have an eleven month old girl, a real sweetie pie. I knew her from the Mologne House. She woke up around midnight and was crying. The father, who was injured in Iraq, not an amputee, yelled at her to, "knock it off". He kept yelling and the more he yelled the more she cried. The mother, who is a young girl, took her to the family room. I got up and made myself a cup of tea, tried talking to the mother, and tried rocking the baby to sleep. That did not do any good and when she took the baby back to their room, she started crying again. And he started yelling again. I remember his Mother, who has since gone home, and I remember that he was very mean to her, more than normal. All of the Soldiers here get cranky and snappy with their Moms or their spouses, but he was really bad, apparently he still is. He doesn't come out of his room at all, ever. He needs help and he needs to learn how to treat people he supposedly loves. I ended up talking to a couple of people today about him. I found out that last night was actually not as bad as it usually is, and it was bad. I don't know what will happen but hopefully someone will do something.

I know I rambled about that situation but I had a great day here at Fisher House. I spent the day at the hospital with Brian. He finally got the pain under control late this morning. The damned nurse let his nerve block run out and that is why he was in such pain. Anyway, I went back to the Fisher House and relaxed a bit by having a massage. They have a couple come in every Wednesday and do chair massages free of charge. It was wonderful and just what my poor tired sore body needed. I was hurting bad this morning after all I did yesterday. Then some of us cooked dinner together. We had a very nice time. The food was good and the company was great. It's nice to feel normal again. I can't wait for Brian to come here from the hospital. I hope he likes it.

I'm still pretty tired and the room is still a mess. I didn't do anything to it today. I am waiting to see what Brian wants to do with it all.

That's about it here. I'm going to get in my jammies and relax for the rest of the night.

Love,
Roberta

I wish I knew what happened to that couple in the room next door. Other people had spoken about him to social workers and staff at the hospital. I know that they tried to get him into counseling and I don't know if they were successful, but they were asked to move out of the Fisher House shortly after I went home. Brian and Mary both told me that he was not a nice guy.

It's funny how I formed "relationships" with so many people there. Some of them were very brief, but very meaningful – parents of sick children, parents of injured Soldiers, and some of the Soldiers themselves, especially the ones that did not have family with them. They all wanted to have someone to talk to. And so did I.

Thu, 28 Sep 2006 19:30

Hi everyone,

Today started out very hard, but ended on a good note. That is what gives me the strength to face another day here. Brian was in a lot of pain this morning when I got to the hospital. I immediately asked for some Percoset pills for him. I knew they would give him some relief, even if temporary. They did, and he slept for a while, which is what he needs, even though he doesn't know it.

This afternoon he was up to getting out of bed and going down to PT for a while. He did some arm bike exercises and some leg lifts with his right leg. While there, Carrie took off his bandages and put on a shrink sock. His stump is pretty swollen but looks very good. I was very impressed with how it looked compared to a week ago. It was good that he got out of bed and did what he did. When we got back to his room, his mental health doctor came by and he talked with her for a while. My poor guy. He feels guilty because he thinks that he has disrupted my life and his Dad's life and pretty much everyone's life. There is no way to change his mind about that either, so we learn to cope with it.

I can't remember if I told you all about these books that Brian got. They are from the author, Gary Trudeau, who writes the Doonesbury cartoons. He wrote two books in cartoon style about a Soldier who lost his leg in Iraq. It is amazing and so on the money about what it is like to be a Soldier who lost a limb. I cannot remember the title, but if you go online and Google Gary Trudeau, you will find it. You have to read it. It's amazing. And while you are at it, there is an article in Time magazine this week about a reporter who was in Iraq and lost a hand saving Soldiers from a grenade. He came to Walter Reed and stayed at Ward 57. Please read that as well. And get his book if you can. So class, that is your assignment, to read both of these authors, and their works about amputees. (For those who want to read the books, here is the information: *"The Long Road Home"* by G.B. Trudeau ISBN 0-7407-5385-1 and *"The War Within – One More Step At A Time"* by G.B. Trudeau ISBN 0-7407-6202-8). It will give you so much insight to what life is like here. And there will be a test on Monday. LOL.

So I will be home on Saturday. I have resigned myself to the fact that Brian will be alone until Monday when his Dad comes. I am hoping that he stays in the hospital until then. If he stays in, I have a network of people checking in on him while he is there. And if he gets discharged, I also have another network of people who will help him out until Paul comes on Monday. It's nice to be so connected.

The fund raiser for him is on Sunday at 1:00 pm at the Whitman VFW on Essex Street in Whitman. It is at the outdoor pavilion because it holds more people so dress for the weather. There is a roof so you won't get wet, but if it's chilly, be prepared. If anyone wants to bake anything, Cass is having a bake sale table at the raffle.

I know he will love it here at the Fisher House. Brian and Mary will be fine here. It will be a good place for them.

The baby next door is crying right now. I don't hear any yelling though and that is good. I spoke to people in the hospital, people at the Fisher House, and Army people about him, so I think I covered all the bases. I hope so, but I really don't have the strength or energy to deal with it. If things get bad, I will do what is necessary. I hope not, but I will.

So that is my story and I am sticking to it. I think I may have rambled, and I am sorry. I will keep letting you all know what is going on with Brian, but there won't be any first hand information. We move to another chapter in the story of Brian.

Sweet Dreams and Love,
Roberta

It was hard to see him in so much pain. It made me so angry that he had to suffer like that. The nursing staff did the best they could, and they responded to any requests from Brian or me, but they were pretty much overwhelmed. There was always "no room" in the hospital because so many injured Soldiers were there recovering.

I was having a very hard time thinking about leaving him. I wanted to cancel my flight several times. As it was, I changed it to Sunday so I could be with him one more day. It was one less day he would be alone. I don't know why Paul could not come until Monday. I think he wanted to be at the fund raiser as well. I just know that I was sure that he would need me to be with him, and that he should not be alone. I underestimated him, but that is my job, I'm his Mom.

Sat, 30 Sep 2006 13:39

Hi all,

It's Saturday afternoon. It has been quite a rough couple of days here at Walter Reed. Brian has been in a lot of pain. They took the nerve block out yesterday, and I can't figure out why. Then this morning he work up with a fever of 102. They had done some cultures on pieces of the bone they removed and it was infected, and now there is another infection. They have isolated a couple of bugs but don't know where he got them – either from the hospital itself or the public when he was an outpatient. It makes a difference on how he gets treated. They have infectious disease specialists working on him now trying to nip it in the bud. He is petrified of losing more of his leg, especially the knee.

Needless to say, I am a basket case. I am leaving tomorrow and his father can't come until Monday. I feel guilty leaving him like this, but I want to be home for the fund raiser also. And work is expecting me back on Monday. This morning I locked myself out of my room at the Fisher House. What a pain that was. I still have to pack all my stuff because I won't be back except for quick visits. And I am sooooo tired.

So if you come to the fund raiser tomorrow, don't be surprised to find me sleeping in a corner somewhere, or not even there.

I know he is in the best place right now, especially tomorrow when he will be alone. I have asked some of my friends here and some of the nursing techs to keep an eye on him. But please, keep him in your prayers.

Love,
Roberta

I was really falling apart. I did not know it at the time, but I was. I was having panic attacks about leaving him. It was the hardest thing that I ever did, getting on that plane and coming home. I cried like an idiot for most of the flight home. I'm sure people were wondering what the heck my problem was.

The fund raiser was amazing. The guys from the American Legion worked so hard to make it a success, and it was. Chet was a commander for the Legion for two years and I got to know a lot of the guys. They do a lot of good work, especially for the veterans. My whole family came to it, including my sister and her husband who live in Florida. It was a special day, full of laughter and tears. It was hard for me to accept that everyone was there because of my son, because of what happened to him.

Sun, 1 Oct 2006 19:13

Hi all,

I wanted to let you know that I talked with Brian around 7:00 pm. He was fever free and he thinks they isolated the bug that is plaguing him. They started a new antibiotic and I am praying that it does the job. He was so sorry to miss the fund raiser. I told him how wonderful it was to see everyone there. It was a special day and I want him to know that. I want to thank you all for coming. It means the world to me that you all care so much.

I'm so tired right now, I am not sure if I am making sense. I am going to go to bed now and sleep for a very long time.

Thank you all sooooo much.

Love,
Roberta

Tue, 3 Oct 2006 17:05

Hi everyone,

Brian is not well right now. He is having another surgery tomorrow. They did a cat scan on his left leg last night and there is something in there in the front of his leg. It could be an abscess, but they can't tell for sure so they are going to go in and find out. His white blood cell count is low so they may do a transfusion. He looked so pale and drawn when I left him Saturday night, like when he first got there. He is still in considerable pain, but they took him off his Dilaudid at his insistence. I don't know what they are going to do tomorrow for the pain.

Paul took him out of the hospital for several hours today. I guess he brought him back to the Fisher House because he hasn't seen his room yet. I don't think it was a good idea, but what do I know. I'm about ready to hop in a plane and head back to DC. If things don't get better in a day or say, I may just do that.

So please, keep him in your prayers.

Love,
Roberta

It was hard for me to not call the airline and book a flight. I was so worried about him and I hated not being there.

Wed, 4 Oct 2006 10:44

Hi everyone,

Paul just called. It was a big blood clot that was building up in his tissue. Like a blood blister, probably from the Coumidin. They drained it and it looks good. That may be the problem with the white blood cells too, so they will check him for that later.

Paul said there were so many other doctors and therapists waiting in his room for word. They are all concerned about him and really care what happens to him.

I feel a big load off my shoulders now. Maybe I can get some work done now!! Thanks for the prayers.

Love,
Roberta

Wed, 4 Oct 2006 17:38

Hi all,

I just wanted to share this with all of you. Brian just called and you would not believe the difference in his voice. It's loud, strong, and clear again. Not like it has been for a while. He is pain free and feels great. He can't even believe the difference. He said they took two Styrofoam cups full of blood clots from his leg. No wonder he was in so much pain. He is still on IV antibiotics and as soon as he can switch to oral, he will be discharged, probably in another day or so.

It was so great to hear his voice so strong again. I was really in despair hearing it sound so weak and filled with pain. Not any more though. Yipeeeeeeee!!!!!!!!!!!!

Thanks everyone for your thoughts and prayers.

Love,
Roberta

Tue, 10 Oct 2006 16:07

Hi everyone,

I just wanted to write and let you know that as of last night Brian was still in the hospital. He is pain free and doing well, they just want to be aggressive with his antibiotics. They may discharge him today but he will have to go back in twice a day for a bag of IV antibiotics. I haven't talked with him yet so I don't know what they decided. His Mary will be leaving Kansas on Wednesday morning, headed for DC. She is leaving a little earlier than planned.

I am debating whether to go to New Hampshire for the annual ladies weekend. I wasn't going to, especially to take time from work, but I really feel the need to get away from everything. I may sneak out early Friday and just head up for a couple of days. We usually head up on Wednesday, which kind of makes it more than a weekend doesn't it?!

Anyway, I hope all is well with everyone. I feel very out of touch when I am not in DC, but that could be a good thing. When Mary gets there, I know I will hear more from her.

Keep Brian in your prayers.

Love,
Roberta

Mon, 16 Oct 2006 05:11

Good Morning All,

I hope everyone had a great weekend. I know I did. I went to ladies weekend with my sisters and friends and had a great time. It's always beautiful in New Hampshire this time of year.

I talked with Brian this weekend. He is doing great. His Mary arrived on Thursday and when I talked with them on Saturday, they had her all unpacked. She said everything fits nicely into their room at the Fisher House and she loves it there. She has met a lot of people and they have cooked a few meals already. She seems to enjoy being there. Brian is so happy that she is there with him. He asked me when I was coming to visit. I told him I was planning on giving them some time together.

I didn't ask him any medical details. He seemed happy and I figured if there was a problem he would have let me know. I will talk with him again soon.

The Hanson American Legion has hooked us up with some union carpenters who are going to handicap access our house so Brian can come and visit without crawling into it. They were at the house Saturday and are going to draw up plans to make the entry bigger, remove the hearth in the living room and make the bathroom bigger. I hope to have this done by Thanksgiving when he will be home next. They are doing this at no cost to Chet and me. It is amazing that there are people and organizations out there willing to do these things.

Back to work now. And nothing is working right, as usual.

Love,
Roberta

Tue, 24 Oct 2006 19:34

Hi all,

It's been a while. I hope all is well with everyone. I'm still trying to catch up, but that hasn't happened yet. I will get there some day.

Brian is doing very well. He got the stitches out last week, and the cyst has gone away. He got casted today for the left leg, and got the go ahead to walk with the prosthetic as soon as it is ready – tomorrow or the next day at the latest. He got the go ahead to wean off the methadone and Lyrica, two drugs he has been anxious to be done with. He got the PIC (for the IV antibiotics) taken out yesterday and is back on Coumadin pills instead of the injections he was getting twice a day. All in all it has been a good week for him. He loves having his Mary there with him. She loves it as well. As she puts it, by taking care of him, she is serving her country. That is her away message on the computer and it made me laugh. I love her attitude and the way she looks at things.

My little Haley has been sick for over a week. The doctors have run a couple of tests, but nothing has shown so far. She has lost a couple of pounds and we are keeping a close watch on her for dehydration. Cass took her to the hospital on Sunday for some culture tests on her stools and a urine sample. They tape a bag to her diaper area and when she fills it they pull the tape off. Ouch… The poor pumpkin. Hopefully, it is just a stomach virus and will pass soon. She seems ok otherwise and makes me smile so much. She is such a happy baby.

Otherwise, things are good here. The weather is cooler which makes the Jacuzzi much nicer. I never thought I would see the day when I wanted winter to come!!

I'm not sure if anything will come of this but HBO wants to do a documentary on Brian. They have contacted him and Brian is thinking about it. The reporter who did such a good story on him in the Patriot Ledger is in DC right now. He spent all day today with Brian following him around to see what his life is like there. He did a good job on the first story so I'm sure the next one will be just as good.

That's about it here. I will keep you updated, but not as frequently. He is due home for Thanksgiving but I'm not sure of the dates yet. I have the urge to go to DC for a weekend before that. I miss him.

Hugs and Love To All,
Roberta

Thu, 26 Oct 2006 17:07

Hi all,

Just a quick update. Really great news. Brian walked today!! He got both prosthetics on and walked with crutches. Then he walked with a cane. Then he walked on his own!!! How amazing is that? Just a little over four months since he lost his legs and he is up and walking again! Mary called me from PT and told me. The two of us were babbling like babies. She said he was grinning from ear to ear and walking circles around everyone!!! I'm so happy for him. I wish I could have been there to see it.

That's if for now. Just wanted to share the news…

Hugs and Love,
Roberta

Brian – a Red Sox fan at a Nationals game in DC

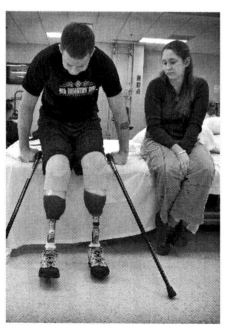

With Mary offering encouragement, and despite setbacks,
Brian resumes his walking

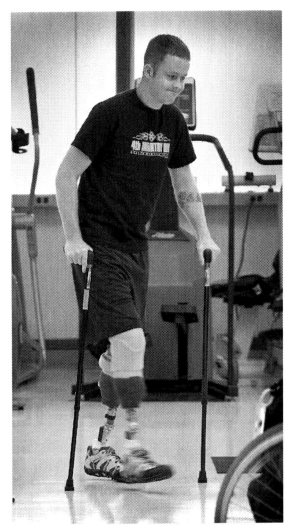

With a look of strong determination, Brian walks again -
just over four months after losing his legs.

Copyright The Patriot Ledger (MA). Photo by Greg Derr. Used with permission.

THE STORY CONTINUES

At that moment, I knew nothing would stop him. I did not know that my belief would be tested sorely in the future. He has gone through many ups and many, many downs throughout this whole ordeal. He continues to ride the roller coaster of recovery. Some days it seems like he takes one step forward and two back. No pun intended.

Brian continued to make progress in therapy. Mary sent pictures of him walking and it was a wonderful sight to see. In November he came home on leave for ten days. It was truly good to see him. He absolutely loved the wheelchair ramp that was built for him. I will always remember the smile on his face as he pushed himself up the ramp. The Veteran's Agent for Hanson, the local carpenters union, the Hanson American Legion, the Whitman American Legion, and the Whitman VFW have done amazing things for Brian. They raised so much money for him and they all want him to join their organizations.

Jordan's Furniture donated a bed for him. I wrote them an email and explained what had happened. We did not have an extra bed here at the house for him to sleep on. They were very generous and responded immediately to my request. Brian loved the bed. He told me it was the first good night's sleep he had had in a long time. He said the one at the Fisher House was pretty uncomfortable. A few months ago, I wrote a letter to a large mattress company and told them about how most of the mattresses were old and worn out. I wrote about how the wounded warriors who were staying at the Fisher House deserved to get a good night's sleep. I told them that they needed a good night's sleep to help them heal and recover from their wounds. I don't know if my letter is what spurred them, because they never wrote back to me, but Brian told me the other day that brand new mattresses were donated to the Fisher House for all of the rooms. The house has eleven rooms, some have double beds and some twins. I like to think that I had something to do with them getting those good mattresses.

Brian became somewhat of a celebrity. He had done a radio talk show, was on the Bill O'Reilly Show, and had several interviews and articles in the local and Boston papers. The local paper did an excellent job on the interviews that they did with him here at home, and with Mary and him in DC. The pictures they took were great. The photographer who took them won an award for one of the pictures. HBO wanted to do a movie on him and his experience. At first he considered it but then changed his mind. He wanted his life to become as normal as possible. Doing that would not have made that happen.

Brian came home for an early Thanksgiving visit. We had a family Thanksgiving dinner at my sister Robin's house. We forgot to bring Brian's crutches so he could get in and out of the house without using the wheelchair. Most home doors are not wide enough for a wheelchair. It also made it impossible for him to move around in her house. He was not able to walk to the bathroom. My nephew's girlfriend went somewhere and borrowed a pair of crutches so he could get around. I was grateful to her for doing that.

It was a bit strange being around the family. Everything seemed different and it's hard to explain. I felt like I was out of touch with them. I think because I had been so focused on Brian for the previous five months that I did not know what was going on in all of their lives. I have five sisters and two brothers. I sort of felt like I "forgot" how to be a sister. I remember feeling like that with Chet, forgetting what it was like to be a wife. I had been a Mom, an aide, a nurse, and a secretary to someone who needed me, and that's all I could handle. When I came home from DC for the last time, I was also exhausted. It took me a long time to "catch my breath".

I also took on the responsibility of taking care of Mary's dog, Bodhran. She obviously could not keep him in DC with them – no dogs allowed. They asked me if I would take care of him until they got back here, and I agreed. I was not too keen on it, but I knew that Mary needed to know he was going to be ok. She would need her strength taking care of Brian.

For the most part, it has worked well. He is a young playful dog and Chet and I aren't as young as we used to be. I felt awful because he developed Lyme disease while here. He was treated for it and is doing well now. It's hard on him when they come to visit. He loves being with Mary and he and Brian get along great. When they leave to go back to DC, he gets very depressed. He mopes around for days, and I really feel bad because I know he is missing his Mary...

Brian began to have problems with infections. He developed a staph infection in the left leg. He also had a bad reaction to some new meds he was put on, causing him to have blood in his urine. He was bitterly disappointed with these setbacks and I was as well. They had scheduled surgery for him to go in and clean up his wound but he ended up not having to have it. It began to clear up with the antibiotics. That was a relief to all of us.

I was having a very hard time at this point. I was having separation anxiety and was worried sick about him. It was very hard not being there and getting all this information first hand. Mary was great in keeping me informed but it just was not the same. I cried at the drop of a hat and had very little control over my emotions. I would be driving down the street, or sitting at work, or grocery shopping, and my mind would just play this image I had of him being blown up in that Humvee. I would see him lying in a hole and looking down to realize that he had no feet. I would see blood, sweat, smoke, the anguish and pain on his face... It was strange and frightening and it made me cry every time it happened.

I decided that it was time for me to find a therapist to help me deal with this. I handled myself well, at least I thought I did, during the crisis and when he needed me, but I was now falling apart. I found someone great. I was lucky because it's not always a sure thing. She helped me regain control of my emotions and my life. It didn't take long, but I know if I had not gone to her, I might never get control of my life.

This was also the time when I decided to write about this whole experience. I had saved the email updates and thought it would be a good place to start. I have come to realize that the writing of this book is therapy for me. For the life of me, I cannot understand why I have the need to want the whole world to know what happened to my son. But I do.

I would go grocery shopping at the local supermarket and hope that I ran into someone I had not seen in a long time so I could tell them about Brian. I would come up with ways to contact someone I had not talked to or seen in a while so I could tell them about him. I thought it was weird, but my therapist told me it wasn't. She said it was a form of therapy for me. I'm happy to say that I have come to grips with all of this and I am now moving forward. I still cry a lot, but most of my tears are tears of joy and tears of pride and love – for all that he has been through and all that he has accomplished.

Brian and Mary spent Christmas in Kansas with Mary's family. I was really ok with that because first, I know Mary gave up a lot to be with him, and second, I was used to Brian not being home for the holidays. His infections were not bothering him and he seemed to be healing. They had a great time and Brian enjoyed meeting Mary's friends and family.

When they got back to DC, he focused on learning to walk. He began wearing a "shrinker" on his left leg to shape it and help with the swelling. After a few days, three areas erupted around the suture line. He was so angry and frustrated. The doctors did not know what was causing this to happen. They took cultures of his leg to find out. The cultures showed nothing, he went back on antibiotics, and began healing again.

Haley's first birthday was approaching. It was hard to believe that she was one year old. She really was my "tonic". I loved just looking at her, playing with her, or rocking her to sleep. She was a big part in keeping me sane.

In March, Brian stood up on two legs. He had to be careful with the left leg, so that it would not "break down" again, but he was so excited to stand on two legs. That was March 1. By March 9, the infection was back again. He was put on antibiotics and was frustrated, as you can imagine. In between this, they went to Vail, Colorado with the Adaptive Sports Program. Because of the infection, Brian could not ski standing up but he did ski using a bucket ski. He had a great time and I think it was the best thing for the both of them to get away from Walter Reed for a while.

He ended up having surgery on March 22. They did a slight revision and took less than an inch off his leg. They took bone samples to have them tested for infection. He not only had the staph infection back, but also had osteomyelitis, an infection of the bone. That was not good news at all. It is very difficult to treat bone infection. He was in the hospital for a longer period than usual. He was allowed to go back to the Fisher House but had to have twice daily IV antibiotics treatments for six weeks. It did the trick though because the infection finally went away, and he got a clean report on his bone scans.

Brian took a short visit to Texas with Mary. He wanted to be there in December 2006 when his unit came back from Iraq. He wanted to be part of the Welcome Home celebration that takes place in Starker Gym at Ft. Hood. He wasn't able to get there in time for that, but he was very happy to see all the "guys". Brian suffered from "survivor's guilt". He knew a lot of men in his unit that were not coming home and would never come home. He also felt guilty that his unit was in Iraq fighting under some extremely harsh conditions while he was home in air conditioning, traveling to Vail, and eating good food. He was surprised to find out that they felt guilt because they thought they let him down. He drew strength from that visit and carries that with him always. He is a proud Soldier of the 4th Infantry Division and you can see that with everything that he does and all that he is.

At the end of April I went to DC with my best friend, Ellen, Brian's godmother. Paul, Brian's Dad, was also there that weekend. We had a great time visiting Brian and Mary. Their room at the Fisher House was decorated and comfy for the two of them. We did some sightseeing and just some visiting and talking.

I showed Ellen around the huge hospital complex and the grounds. I felt so much better after spending a couple of days with them. I saw firsthand how well they were both doing. It put my mind at ease.

Brian continued to do physical therapy and work hard. In May, he took his 30 day convalescent leave. They spent two weeks in Kansas, and then two weeks here. In Kansas they went fishing and camping and Brian drove a car for the first time since his injury. He loved it! He was home here on June 8 and wanted to celebrate the one year anniversary of being wounded. He calls it his "Alive Day". That is truly what it is. We had an open house celebration the entire day.

He came home for another visit in August 2007. It was amazing watching him walk without the aid of a walker or crutches. He still has some work to do with his gait and balance, but I never saw him use the wheelchair the whole time he was here. Well, actually he did use it. He used it to push Haley around in the driveway. LOL.

He will always need the wheelchair. It will be a part of him for the rest of his life. There will be days when his stumps hurt and he won't be able to wear his legs. He'll also need it for getting in and out of the shower and for days when he is just tired. But I will never, ever grow tired of watching him walk. He plays with Haley, chasing after her. He went to the batting cages and swung a bat. He went boating in Boston Harbor. He wrestled with Cassie, just like he always has. He is my son, my smiling friend. And he is alive.

Nothing in my life could have prepared me for this ordeal. I have no words to describe it. It was horrifying from the moment I received that call until the present day. I learned of how my son battled back from almost dying in Iraq, and basically saving his own life. I saw the strength and the courage he possesses first hand. I learned that I was stronger than I ever thought possible, and that I would do anything for my children, and their children.

It's been over a year now since that day. Brian is still at Walter Reed. He has had setbacks, including a very serious bone infection that was difficult to treat. He has been skiing in Vail and loved every minute of it. He expects to be there just another few months and is very anxious to be out of Walter Reed and to begin his life back home. The organization, Homes For Our Troops, is going to build him a completely handicapped accessible home in Plymouth, MA. He will be close to me and the rest of the family. Mary and Brian have set a wedding date. They decided to get married on the anniversary of Brian's injury, June 8, 2008. Brian wants a happy memory for that day.

My son is alive...

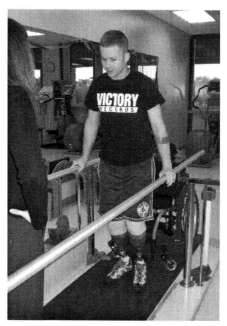

Continued PT – November 2006

Brian in Boston – December 2006

MY SON IS ALIVE...

Brian – looking good in uniform – April 2007

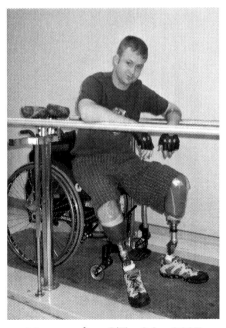

Never ending PT – May 2007

Alive Day Celebration – June 8, 2007

Progress continues – bicycle rider – July 2007

Who would have thought – rock climbing – July 2007 – less than 14 months after being wounded

THE STORY CONTINUES

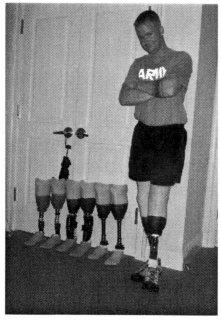

Posing with legs for all occasions – August 2007

Enjoying a boat ride with niece, Haley – August 2007

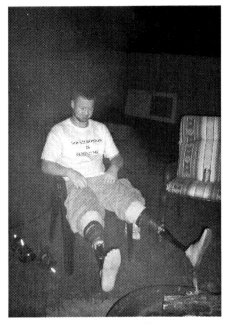

Brian said, "My feet are cold" – August 2007

Batting cage – August 2007

Groundbreaking for Brian's house being built by
Homes for Our Troops – September 21, 2007

Roberta, Brian, and Mary – happy at the groundbreaking ceremony

INTERNET LINKS OF INTEREST

The following links are provided to give additional information on some of the resources available to wounded warriors and to those wanting to read more about Brian's unit:

Active duty 4th Infantry Division – official web site of the 4th Infantry Division. http://pao.hood.army.mil/4ID/

Aleethia Foundation - www.aleethia.org

Homes for our Troops – www.homesforourtroops.org

National 4th Infantry Division (4ID) Association – organization supporting veterans of the 4ID. www.4thinfantry.org

Red Cross – www.redcross.org

Wounded Warrior Project – www.woundedwarriorproject.org

Yellow Ribbon Fund - www.yellowribbonfund.com

Brian is very proud of his 66th Armor Regiment and the 4th Infantry Division, parent unit of the Regiment. Following are brief histories of those historic units:

HISTORY OF 66TH ARMOR REGIMENT

The 66th Armor Regiment is the oldest Armor unit in the United States Army, tracing its lineage to the beginning of the Tank Service in February 1918. The Regiment participated in the battles of St. Mihiel, France, where it received its baptism of fire, and in the Meuse-Argonne and the Somme Offensives.

The numerical designation of the Regiment was changed several times during the period of 1918 to 1928. On 15 July 1940, the unit was re-designated from the 66th Infantry (Light Tanks) to the 66th Armor Regiment as part of the newly formed 2nd Armored Division, stationed at Ft. Benning, GA.

In December 1942, the Regiment participated in the amphibious invasion of French Morocco in North Africa and led the Division's triumphant entry into Casablanca. The Regiment also participated in the invasion of Sicily.

In June 1944, the Regiment went into action on the European Continent, landing on Normandy's beaches soon after D-Day. They earned the Presidential Unit Citation for their actions in the St. Lo breakout in late July and early August 1944. The 66th Armor Regiment rolled across France to the German border. It was diverted north to counter the German advance during the battle of the Bulge. During World War II, the 66th earned seven battle streamers.

The Regiment and other units of the 2nd Armored Division were selected to occupy Berlin and serve as the first American troops to enter the fallen German Capital.

During the Korean War, an offspring of the 66th fought under the designation "6th Tank Battalion". During the war, the Sixth won seven battle streamers and the Korean Presidential Unit

Citation. These honors were awarded to the 66th Armor Regiment when the 6th Tank Battalion was deactivated after the conflict.

During the Cold War, the Regiment spent time serving in Germany and in Fort Hood, TX, always ready to meet the Soviet threat to the European continent.

In 1991, elements of the 66th Armor Regiment deployed to the Kingdom of Saudi Arabia in support of operation Desert Shield and fought in Desert Storm. During Desert Storm the Regiment again proved its worth by assisting in the liberation of Kuwait and the push towards Iraq.

In December 1995, when the 2nd Armored Division was deactivated, two battalions of the 66th Armor Regiment transferred to become part of the 1st Brigade Combat Team of the 4th Infantry Division. For the next seven years, they were part of the test element for the Army, Force XXI, testing tactics, communications, electronics, organization, and weapons to lead the Army into the 21st century.

In late March 2003, the 66th Armor deployed to Kuwait and in April, along with other 1st Brigade Combat Team units, led the 4th Infantry Division into the Sunni Triangle of Iraq where they fought in Operation Iraqi Freedom I until March 2004. Among the brigade's accomplishments was the capture of Saddam Hussein and award of a Valorous Unit Citation.

After training and reorganizing at Fort Hood, TX during the last half of 2004 and 2005, the unit again deployed to Iraq in late 2005 for another year long tour in the Sunni Triangle, this time serving in Taji, northwest of Baghdad. As this book goes to press, the 1st Battalion, 66th Armor Regiment is preparing for their third deployment to Iraq, in December 2007.

HISTORY OF 4TH INFANTRY DIVISION

The 4th Infantry Division (4ID) is nicknamed the "Ivy Division." This comes from the design of the shoulder sleeve insignia which has four green ivy leaves joined at the stem and opening at the four corners. The word "Ivy" is a play on the Roman numeral four, IV. Ivy leaves are symbolic of tenacity and fidelity, the basis of the Division's motto, "Steadfast and Loyal."

The 4ID has a long and distinguished history that includes combat in four wars. Sixteen Ivy Division Soldiers have been awarded the Congressional Medal of Honor and 21 campaign streamers adorn its colors. Additionally, we honor four Soldiers of other units who were awarded the Medal of Honor while their units were attached to the 4ID. The division was formed in December 1917, and was commanded by Maj. Gen. George H. Cameron. Following the United States entry into World War I, the division embarked for Europe as part of the American Expeditionary Force.

The 4ID went into action in the Aisne-Marne campaign in July 1918, at which time its units were piecemealed and attached to several French infantry divisions. Almost a month later, the division was reunited for the final days of the campaign. During the next four months, the 4ID saw action on the front lines and reserves. Suffering more than 11,500 casualties in the final drive for the Allied victory, the 4ID was the only division to serve in the French, British and American sectors of the front.

The American people once again called upon the 4ID to serve in World War II. From staging areas in England, the division trained for its major role in Operation Overlord (D-Day) — the amphibious invasion of Europe on June 6, 1944. The division's 8th Infantry Regiment was the first Allied unit to assault German forces on the Normandy Coast.

The remainder of the division quickly followed, landing on Utah Beach. For 26 days, the division pushed inland, reaching the Port of Cherbourg and sustaining more than 5,000 casualties in the first month of fighting.

Breaking out of the beachhead and expanding operations well into France, the division led the St. Lo breakout, and was the first Allied unit into Paris. The division quickly moved on through northern France, reaching Belgium and the border of Germany by September 1944. On September 11, 1944, a patrol of the 4ID became the first Allied ground force to enter Germany. Fighting on the Siegfried Line followed. In November, the division moved into the Hurtgen Forest and fought what was to be its fiercest battle. The 4ID held its ground during the Battle of the Bulge, securing the southern shoulder of the Bulge in Luxembourg; crossed the Rhine, then the Danube, and finally ceased its advance at the Isar River in southern Germany. The division suffered almost 22,000 battle casualties and over 34,000 total casualties, including over 5,000 who were killed, during their eleven months of fighting across Europe. For 199 straight days, the 4ID was in constant contact with the Germans.

The Cold War found the 4ID again standing tall in defense of freedom. While others fought the Communists in Korea, the Ivy Division returned to Germany in 1950 and for the next six years stood strong against the Soviet threat in Western Europe. After returning to the States in 1956, the division trained at Fort Lewis, Washington, for the next time they would be called into battle.

In 1966, the 4ID again saw combat, this time in Vietnam. Led in August by the 2nd Brigade, the Ivy Division headquarters closed into the central highlands of Vietnam on September 25, 1966. Their combat assignment against the North Vietnamese did not end until December 7, 1970. Eleven additional battle streamers would be added to the 4ID colors as the Ivy Division Soldiers fought in places such as the Ia Drang Valley, Plei Trap Valley, Fire Base Gold, Dak To, the Oasis, Kontum, Pleiku, Ben Het, An Khe, and Cambodia. Over 15,000 4ID Soldiers were wounded and almost 2,500 killed in Vietnam.

The 4ID returned from Vietnam in December 1970 and settled at Fort Carson, Colorado, where it reorganized as a mechanized infantry division and remained at Carson for 25 years. It was during the division's time at Fort Carson that it picked up the unofficial nickname of the "Ironhorse" Division. The 4ID moved its colors to Fort Hood, Texas, in December 1995 to become the Army's first "Digitized Division" under the Force XXI program. In this program, the division was thoroughly involved in the training, testing and evaluation of 72 initiatives to include the Division's Capstone Exercise (DCX) I held at the National Training Center in Fort Irwin, California, in April 2001 and culminating in the DCX II held at Fort Hood in October 2001.

Division elements have supported rotations to Bosnia and Kuwait as well as providing a Task Force to fight forest fires in Idaho in 2000. 4ID Soldiers supported the Winter Olympics in Utah. Since November 2001, the division's mission was the Division Ready Brigade – prepared to deploy at a moment's notice to anywhere in the world.

In January 2003, the division received orders to support Operation Iraqi Freedom. The entire division loaded its equipment and deployed to war in Iraq. Arriving in March 2003, the division moved from its Kuwaiti staging areas northward to an area north of Baghdad. Division headquarters was established in Tikrit, and the division's brigades were located over a large Area of Operations in the "Sunni Triangle." Thousands of raids and patrols were launched to find remnants of Saddam Hussein loyalists and terrorist operatives who were in the area. One important accomplishment of the division was the capture of Saddam Hussein, the former president of Iraq, on 13 December 2003. He was found just south of Tikrit, hiding in a spider-hole. In addition to the wartime and counter-insurgency missions, the division was instrumental in opening and supplying thousands of schools, hospitals and clinics within its AO. Division personnel also repaired bridges, roads, power plants, oil pipelines, water mains and many other essential parts of the Iraqi infrastructure.

Returning to Fort Hood in March 2004, the division reset more than 71,000 pieces of equipment, making it the first division to fully reset its entire formation after a year of combat while simultaneously transforming. Reset included modernizing all weapon systems and standardizing the fleets. By reorganizing, the division led the way for the Army in modularizing a heavy division. The 4ID is now made up of four brigade combat team's that are each self-sufficient, each with a tactical force of approximately 3,600 Soldiers.

The 4ID's latest deployment was OIF 05-07. The entire division of more than 21,000 Soldiers deployed to Iraq to conduct decisive full-spectrum combat operations in support of the combatant commander objectives. Task Force Ironhorse met Army strategic objectives as Multi-National Division – Baghdad by training nine Iraqi police brigades and ten Iraqi army brigades to secure their own country. Additionally, the Ironhorse Division destroyed more than 500 weapons caches, including more than 8,300 pounds of explosives, 2,000 rockets, 4,700 mortar rounds and production materials for roadside bombs, making the battlefield safer for American forces and Iraqi citizens. Throughout these operations, ground forces killed or detained 120 high-value targets, including Abu Musab al-Zarqawi, dealing a serious blow to insurgent operations. Task Force Ironhorse also completed more than 1,000 civic action projects, including 146 water and sewage projects, 145 road improvement projects, and 37 major agriculture projects that invested $580 million into the Iraqi economy.

Today, the 4ID is training for its third deployment to Iraq. As a team, the 4ID is focused on reset, reintegrate, retrain and prepare for redeployment. The division is a split-based command, with two Brigade Combat Teams at Fort Carson, Colorado and two Brigade Combat Teams and Division Headquarters at Fort Hood, Texas. The 4ID headquarters and 1st and 3rd Brigade Combat Teams will return to Iraq for their third rotation in December 2007. Other 4ID units have been alerted for deployment and will return to Iraq sometime during 2008.

BOOKS BY DEEDS PUBLISHING

"War Stories – Utah Beach to Pleiku" by Robert O. Babcock. 450 personal war stories from veterans of the 4th Infantry Division from WWII (325 stories), Cold War (25 stories), and Vietnam (100 stories). 700 pages, soft cover. ISBN 0-9776018-1-1. $34.95

"Operation Iraqi Freedom I – A Year in the Sunni Triangle" by Robert O. Babcock. The history of the 4th Infantry Division and Task Force Ironhorse in Iraq – April 2003 to April 2004, including a chapter on the capture of Saddam Hussein. 369 pages, hard cover. ISBN 0-9710551-8-1. $29.95

"What Now, Lieutenant?" by Robert O. Babcock. The personal account of Bob Babcock's experiences as a platoon leader and executive officer with Bravo Company, 1st Battalion, 22nd Infantry Regiment, 4th Infantry Division in Vietnam in 1966 and 1967. 426 pages, soft cover. ISBN 0-9776018-0-3. $29.95

"The Sooner the Better" by John E. Tatum. A former Oklahoma University football player, whose no-nonsense management style merged three successful Farm Bureau Companies into the $1.4 billion Farm Bureau Mutual Insurance Company. John tells his personal story of achievement spiced with advice on attitude, education, and life in general – a great read for anyone with ambition. 170 pages, soft cover. ISBN 0-9776018-2-X. $17.95

"You Don't Know Jack… or Jerry" by Robert O. Babcock. In thirty years, Jack Henry and Jerry Hall have grown their banking software company from the two of them to an operation with over 3,500 employees and $650 million in revenue. There is nothing more American than a couple of small-town guys with an idea, who take the idea, nurture it, and work hard to make it happen. The story of Jack Henry and Associates is one every business entrepreneur not afraid to dream can aspire to match. 264 pages, hard cover. ISBN 0-9776018-3-8. $28.00

Order all books from www.deedspublishing.com.

ABOUT THE AUTHOR

Roberta Quimby still lives in the small town of Hanson, Massachusetts, south of Boston, where she grew up and raised her two children. While working her daily job, she is actively involved in her children's lives, taking joy each day from her granddaughter Haley's smiles. She continues to support our military and hopes to raise awareness of the plight of our American Soldiers returning from Iraq and Afghanistan.

Brian will hopefully be discharged from the Army late in 2007 and return to civilian life. All of the steps Roberta and Brian have taken since that day in Iraq have led them down a road many, many other Soldiers and their families have traveled. They will continue on with strength and determination that neither of them knew they had. The memories will fade but they will never completely go away. Roberta hopes that when Brian's new home is built, he will finally have some peace and that they all cannot only be grateful he is alive, but start making some new memories to hopefully replace some of the old ones – some new wonderful experiences that all military families deserve.